# SPEECH ACT AND LINGUISTIC COMMUNICATION

## About the Author

**Rishikant Pandey** (*b.* 1967) completed his Master Degree in Philosophy from University of Allahabad with the first rank in the first class in 1991 and was awarded by *Nirmal Chand Mukharjee Gold Medal*. Soon after, he received U.G.C. Research Fellowship and completed his D.Phil. Degree in 1999. He was appointed lecturer in 1996 and presently he is Reader in Philosophy, Allahabad Degree College, a constituent college of Allahabad University. He is a life member of various philosophical organizations, like Indian Philosophical Congress; Akhil Bhartiya Darshan Parishad; and Uttar Bharat Darshan Parishad. He has published numerous articles in the leading philosophical journals, like *Indian Philosophical Quarterly* and *Journal of Indian Council of Philosophical Research*. His other book is *Darshnik Vimarsh*.

# SPEECH ACT AND LINGUISTIC COMMUNICATION

Rishikant Pandey

CONCEPT PUBLISHING COMPANY, NEW DELHI-110 059

**Cataloging in Publication Data—DK**
*Courtesy:* D.K. Agencies (P) Ltd. <docinfo@dkagencies.com>

**Pandey, Rishikant,** 1967-
Speech act and linguistic communication / Rishikant Pandey.
p. cm.
Includes bibliographical references (p. )
Includes index.
ISBN 13: 9788180695131
ISBN 10: 8180695131

1. Speech acts (Linguistics). 2. Communication. 3. Analysis (Philosophy). 4. Language and languages—Philosophy. 5. Austin, J. L. (John Langshaw), 1911-1960. I. Title.

DDC 401.4 22



ISBN-13: 978-81-8069-513-1
ISBN-10: 81-8069-513-1

First Published 2008



*Published and Printed by*
Ashok Kumar Mittal
**Concept Publishing Company**
A/15-16, Commercial Block, Mohan Garden
New Delhi (INDIA)

*Phones* : 25351460, 25351794
*Fax* : 091-11-25357103
*Email* : publishing@conceptpub.com

# Foreword

Since Plato western philosophy has been engaged in the task of examining the nature and power of analysis and the predominant view till the neo- Hegelian thought was that analysis gives only a distorted view of reality. Bradley may be recalled as the last important champion of this view point. Bertrand Russell, who was closely associated with Bradley during the earlier period of his philosophizing, reversed the idealistic position by holding that analyse reveals reality. Reality, however, has a different meaning in the analytical movement. Reality here is the reality in Wittgensteinian sense which finds its most forceful explanation in his declarations that language is picture of reality and the world is everything that is the case. Analysis reveals reality in the sense that it acts as a catharsis. Metaphysical language is confusing and misleading and analysis exposes those confusions and clarifies the misleading. Philosophy in its power sense, therefore, is the analysis of language.

The movement of analysis as a philosophy has a long history and this monograph, besides presenting a systematic detail of this history, focuses its attention on the special contribution of the J.L. Austin to movement in the form of the philosophy of language. Austin developed his philosophy of language, popularly known as speech act theory, by making several subtle distinctions in the functioning of language, both verbal and non-verbal. Initially Austin distinguished between the constative and the performative functions of language and maintained that in its former function language say something and in its later function a linguistic utterance is used to perform something. However, Austin soon realized that the inadequacies of this watertight division of the linguistic utterance and formulated his famous speech act theory which is in its simplest form means that language not only describes something but also performs some act.

The author examines the various criticisms against Austin's theory and the alternative explanations and relations to the problem of linguistic communication offered by such philosophers of language as Wittgenstein, Searle, Bach, Chisholm, Max Black, G.J. Warnock, H.P. Grice and others and argues that if we can't properly understand the role of *the intention of the speaker*, the nature and the function of verbal communication can be grasped as simultaneously performing the twin acts of description and stimulation.

How language works? is another great controversial problems among the philosophers of language. Dr. Pandey stems clear of the two polar situation, viz., conventionalization and standardization and stipulates certain conditions for successful communication. Socio-cultural conditions, he argues, may cause problem in communication. Therefore, the conditions necessary to get over this problem are : mutual understanding between the speaker and the hearer, job-orientation between the communicating parties, motivation of the hearer, intention of the speaker and the force of the utterance. The role of these conditions has been explained by drawing examples from various forum of linguistic communication.

Austin argues that *securing of uptakes* is an indispensable factor in successful communication. What it means is that the hearer must be able to recognize the intention of the speaker. It is at this point that non-verbal form of expression plays a significant role. The speaker may hide his intention in verbal expressions but his non-verbal expressions may reveal it. It depends on the hearer's ability, therefore, to correctly understand the meaning of the verbal statements by interpreting the non-verbal behaviour of the speaker. The author has very ably elaborated the importance of non-verbal speech and has tried to substantiate its by making reference to Bhartrihari's philosophy of language. In Bhartrihari's philosophy of language, word has taken to be the ultimate reality and this reality, though the source of all verbal expressions, itself is beyond the touch of language. Is it not possible, therefore, that by recognizing the importance of non-verbal speech the linguistic philosophers are indirectly acknowledging the role of the subject, the experienced, and the knower for any successful communication? This is a question which has not been specially raised by the author but the question silently suggests itself during the course of analysis and discussion. May be metaphysical question of the subject as the ground of all knowledge and communication is not that irrelevant in speech acts as the philosophers of language tend to perceived it. I wish this question is taken up as the sequel to this book by Dr. Pandey or someone else so that a meeting ground may be found between the philosophers of analysis and the metaphysicians.

This book is a result of intensive research of Dr. Pandey. A rich bibliography at the end of the book is of great help to the readers and the researchers. This is certainly a good addition to the existing literature on the analytical philosophy particularly Austin's philosophy of language. I hope the book will be well received by the scholars.

**Prof. Sabhageet Mishra**
*Former Professor and Head*
*Department of Philosophy*
*D.D.U. University, Gorakhpur*

15.06.2007

# Preface

This book is about the development of Analytical philosophy and the contributions made by J.L. Austin and other philosophers, like, R.M. Chisholm, Max Black, L.W. Forguson, Water Cerf, Keith Graham, G.J. Warnock, Mat Furberg, P.F. Strawson, L.J. Cohen, J.R. Searle, K. Bach, R.M. Hernish, H.P. Grice, Mark Platts, S. Blackburn, Alexander Millar and so forth. Initially, joint efforts of Moore and Russell founded a base for Analytical philosophy. They differed, however, in their approaches. On the one hand, Moore believed in ordinary language. Russell, on the other hand, brushed aside ordinary language and argued in the favour of ideal language. Russell contended that our ordinary language is complex, vague, equivocal. We, therefore, can't distinguish its logical and grammatical form. Philosophical problems arise due to the complexity of ordinary language. Hence, only on the basis of ideal language, we can solve the problems of philosophy. Later, the concept of ideal language was also substantiated by early Wittgenstein and Logical positivists.

Although, the trend of ordinary language philosophy began with Moore's contribution nonetheless it was systematically developed by Wittgenstein's in his later formulations. Even in his earlier phase, *i.e.* in *'Tractatus-Logico-Philosophicus'*, Wittgenstein asserted that all propositions of our colloquial language are actually, just as they are, logically completely in order. In his later phase, *i.e.* in *'Philosophical Investigations'* he lucidly conceived that philosophical problems arise when we use our words without considering their proper contexts. If we use our words in their proper contexts, there would be no problem. He, therefore, said that philosophical problem has the form 'I do not know my way about'. Furthermore, philosophical problems arise when language goes on holiday.

Wittgenstein, therefore, was led to the foundation of ordinary language philosophy. Later, this trend was countenanced by numerous Cambridge philosophers and this school is known as *Cambridge school's of ordinary language philosophy*. The trend of ordinary language philosophy also flourished in Oxford. Oxford philosophers, however, conceived ordinary language philosophy with some modification so that it is known as *Oxford school's of ordinary language philosophy*.

Precisely, there are some similarities and dissimilarities between both of the schools. Both are against of ideal language and argue in the favour of ordinary language. Moreover, they contented that philosophical problems arise due to improper applications of language. However, there are some significant differences between the two schools. Wittgenstein's approach was negative. He compared philosophical problems with mental disease while the approach of Oxford philosophers was positive. They conceived that some problems may be like therapeutic but philosophy is mostly constructive so that on the basis of ordinary language we can solve the varied problems of philosophy. Austin, for instance, suggested that the systematic and scientific study of ordinary language is important in itself and therefore, he called it *Linguistic phenomenology* or *expanded science of grammar*. Apart from this, Wittgenstein and other Cambridge philosophers began their philosophical interest with the study of some specific problem, whereas the Oxford philosophers were interested in solving general problems of philosophy.

J.L. Austin substantiated the trend of *Oxford school's of ordinary language philosophy* while saying that in our common stock of language there are so many subtle distinctions involved which we can't understand sitting on an easy armchair. This book critically discusses the Austin's formulation propounded in his book, *'How to Do Things with Words'*, along with the comments raised by varied distinguished philosophers.

This book has nine chapters. The first chapter, *British analytical philosophy*, presents the brief history of analytical philosophy, *i.e.*, how analytical philosophy developed and what was the position of Austin. The second chapter, *Austin's aims and method,* presents that Austin's aim was to develop a new science and thereby he predicted that in future with the collaboration of philosophers, grammarians and the students of language, a new science, *Science of Language,* would emerge. For this purpose, he disowned *idiosyncratic method* and suggested for *co-operative pursuit.* The third chapter, *Constative and performative utterance,* elucidates that initially Austin distinguished between the constative and the performative utterances. The constative utterance is used to say or state something so that it is always either true or false. Whereas, the performative utterance is used to do something so that it is always happy or unhappy *inter alia* true or false. Later on, Austin himself rejected this distinction and argued that each utterance is constative and performative both, *e.g.,* an utterance is not only to say something but also to do something. The fourth chapter, *Why to distinguish between constative and performative utterances?,* delineates that on the basis of *the intention of the speaker* or *circumstances,* it can be shown that the distinction between the constative and the performative utterances are justified. The fifth chapter, *Speech Act Theory,* is considered as *terminal point* or *core enterprise* of his book, *How to Do Things with Words.* Austin began his journey with theoretical formulation by making a distinction between the constative and the performative utterances. Later, he revised this distinction and enunciated that *every speech is an act,* which is known as *Speech Act Theory.* The sixth chapter, *Non-verbal speech act,* deals with the fact that if the job of language is *securing of uptake, viz.,* the hearer not only deems the speaker's intention but also he recognizes it, it can be done non-verbally also. The Speech Act, therefore, may be of three sorts; *Direct Speech Act, Indirect Speech Act,* and *Non-verbal Speech Act.* The seventh chapter, *How performatives really work?,* elucidates how language works. J.R. Searle argued in favour of conventionalization, whereas, K. Bach and R.M. Hernish emphasised on standardization. I have contended that language works in accordance with socio-cultural contexts. Conventionalization and standardization are embedded in the larger socio-cultural context. In the eighth chapter, *Is language adequate for the correct inference of the speaker's intention?*, I have endeavoured to determine the touchstones to judge the speaker's intention. It becomes more intricate when the speaker hides his real intention and reveals his hidden intention. The question is: if the speaker hides his real intention and expressed his hidden intention, what would be the ample criterion to judge his/her real intention? In other words, how intention, language, and behaviour are bound up with each other. Eventually, the concluding chapter, *Epilogue*, presents the seminal thought of this book.

My interest in Analytical Philosophy developed at the Master level course on the subject taught by Prof. D.N. Diwedi, former Head, Department of Philosophy, University of Allahabad, Allahabad. Later, after award of U.G.C. Research Fellowship, when I approached Prof. Diwedi, he kindly agreed to be my doctoral thesis supervisor. Under his supervision, I completed my doctoral thesis on *'A Critical Study of J.L. Austin's Speech Act Theory'* in 1999 at the University of Allahabad. I continued working on the subject and also published research articles in the journals like *Indian Philosophical Quarterly*. This book presents my works of the last one decade representing my earlier and revised formulations including two published research articles.

Last year, while teaching the Contemporary Western Philosophy course of M.A students, I felt that there is no book for M.A. final students, especially on J.L. Austin. Decision to write a book on the Speech Act Theory was partly influenced by my experience of non-availability of a comprehensive book on this subject.

This book is expected to be adopted as a supplementary text for master level course on Analytical Philosophy and it would be advantageous for the scholars of linguistics, communication and of great interest to the general readers.

This is an occasion to express my gratitude and thanks to my teachers, colleagues and all those visible and invisible sources, who directly or indirectly helped me to give a concrete shape of this work. Firstly, I would like to record my sincere gratitude to my spiritual Guru Brahmlin Param Sant Sri R.B. Mathur, whose unseen blessings confer on me extraordinary strength to cope with this arduous and painstaking task. I also express my gratitude to my mentor Prof. D.N. Diwedi for shaping my intellectual pursuits leading to completion of this work and my academic career. I also record my sincere gratitude and thanks to Prof. Sabhajeet Mishra, former Head, Department of Philosophy, D.D.U. University, Gorakhpur, who read the manuscript and enriched me with several valuable suggestions. He has kindly written the foreword of this book. His keen interest, encouragement, academic support and feedback led to the evolution of this work. I would like to record my personal regard to my teachers Prof. S.K. Seth, Prof. R.L. Singh, Prof. Jata Shankar, Prof. Hari Shankar Upadhyay, Prof. M.R. Prakash, Prof. N. Singh, Prof. Gauri Chattopadhyay, Dr. Asha Lal for their encouragement. Prof. Jata Shankar and Prof. Hari Shanker Upadhyay have especially shown keen interest in my present work and they have consistently provided feedbacks and academic support, positively improving quality of my work. I also record my thanks to my friends and colleagues Dr. R.M. Pathak, Dr. S.B. Singh, Dr. Sanjay K. Shukla, Dr. Tanuja Tiwari, and Dr. Anjana Pathak, who were always ready for discussion and deliberations.

I am also grateful to librarians and their staff of various libraries especially of the Indian Council of Philosophical Research, Lucknow, University of Allahabad, Allahabad, and the G.B. Pant Social Science Research Institute, Jhusi for lending me much needed support.

Last but not least, I record my special gratitude and thanks to my parents and my in-laws whose blessings are always with me. I am grateful to my wife Vibha, son Divyanshu and daughter Aditi, without their support, this painstaking task was not possible.

Allahabad **Rishikant Pandey**
19.9.2007

# Contents

# 1

# British Analytical Philosophy

The British Analytical Philosophy which made a beginning in the first half of the 20th century has three main phases. Firstly, before the First World War, two distinguished British Philosophers: B. Russell and G.E. Moore, expounded the great theory of realism in their writings and finally, presented in their books: *Problems of Philosophy* (1912) and *Some Main Problems of Philosophy* (1953), respectively. They set forth their theory against the idealism of Hegel, Bradley, Green and other idealistic philosophers. Prior to Moore and Russell, idealism was on the top position. Its fundamental principle, *i.e.*, the doctrine of the abstract idea was, however, very complex and it was against of common sense knowledge. Hence, philosophy became far from the reach of common man. On this account, Moore and Russell with their joint efforts, endeavoured to build up a doctrine based on empiricism and known as naive realism. However, with the start of the First World War, numerous philosophers got involved in the War. Academic work was, therefore, greatly paralysed.

In the second phase, philosophical method developed in a very different style, which is known as *logical analysis*. In this spell, Russell along with the earlier Wittgenstein enunciated the doctrine of Logical Atomism. This name was given by B. Russell in his lectures during 1918-19 and later on most elaborately propounded by Wittgenstein in his book *Tractatus-Logico-Philosophicus* (1922). Moreover, this process was also accepted by the Logical Positivists, whose prominent members were Schlick, Neurath, and Carnap at Vienna and A.J. Ayer at Oxford. This doctrine is based upon the analysis of language and therefore, it is not concerned with the study of reality. According to the analytical philosophers, it is the job of scientists and not of philosophers to acquire the knowledge of reality. The prime job of philosophers is to analyze only language. As J.O. Urmson wrote, "………they meant something which, whatever precise description of it they choose at least involved the attempt to rewrite in different and in some way more appropriate terms those statements which they found philosophically puzzling."[1]

In the third phase, later phase of Wittgenstein (Latter Wittgenstein) developed a new school of analytical philosophy, known as ordinary language philosophy. Indeed, the trend of ordinary language philosophy begins with G.E. Moore's philosophy. As A.M. Quinton remarked, "Moore was in no sense the leader of this school."[2] However, Wittgenstein was that philosopher who systematically developed ordinary language as a philosophical method. Initially, Wittgenstein argued in the favour of the ideal language (picture theory), which emphasises that language is the symbolic representation of the fact experienced. Later, he felt some problems in this doctrine so that he brushed it aside and advocated another doctrine known as *use theory* or *contextual theory*. This doctrine advocates that there is no certain and definite meaning of a word or a sentence. The meaning of a word varies due to variations of its uses. At that time, Wittgenstein was working at Cambridge. Later on, numerous distinguished Oxford philosophers like G. Ryle, J.L. Austin and P.F. Strawson were greatly impressed by this doctrine and thereby they developed and modified this concept at Oxford, but in different ways.

The tradition of analysis is not a new trend in the history of western philosophy. A number of ancient philosophers were also analysts. One of the first philosophers who initiated this trend, was Socrates. Socrates raised many fundamental questions. For instance, What is justice? What is knowledge? What is good? and the like. When he raised these questions, his chief aim was to analyse the meaning as well as the concepts of these words.

Plato and Aristotle further developed this trend. In his celebrated book *Republic*, Plato wrote, "Whenever a number of individuals have a common name, we assume them to have also a corresponding idea or form."[3] This quote is referring the salient characteristics of language, *i.e.*, whenever there will be a common noun or an adjective, there must be a large number of corresponding objects or things. For instance, cow, tree, pen, wall, house and so forth. These terms necessarily insinuate a thing or a object corresponding in this world. This contention is underpinned over his theory of ideas. Now, it has proved that Plato's doctrine was based on a false presumption. Hence, it can be said that the wrong interpretation of language developed an illusionary philosophical principle.

Similarly, Aristotle in his Metaphysics, Book *Zeta*, Chapter 1, argued, "And so one might even raise the question whether the words, 'to talk', 'to be healthy', 'to sit', imply that each of these things is existent, and similarly in other cases of this sort; for none of them is either self-subsistent or capable of being separated from substance, but rather, if anything, it is that which walks or sits or is healthy that is an existent thing. Now, these are seen to be more real because there is something definite which underlies them (*i.e.*, the substance or individual) which is implied in such a predicate; for we never use the word 'good' or 'sitting' without implying this."[4] Precisely, Aristotle endeavoured to show that we do not use verbs without its corresponding object to the extent that both are bound up to each other. For example, we can't use the word *sit* or *walk* and so on, but we may use the expression like *he is sitting* or *he is walking* and the like. Aristotle, therefore, proved that *substance* or *things* but not activity have their own independent existence. Ontologically, substances are more fundamental than the activity. This theory is, therefore, also hinged upon the process of analysis.

In the modern age, George Berkeley in his book, *Treatise Concerning the Principles of Human Knowledge* also followed this trend. While describing the functions of language, he asserted, ".......the communicating of ideas.......is not the chief and only end of language, as is commonly supposed. There are other ends, as the raising of some passion, the exciting to or deterring from action, the putting the mind in some particular disposition; ....."[5] It delineates that the job of language is not only to communicate an idea but also to express passions, dispositions and so forth. Precisely, this assertion is relied upon the analysis of language. It advocates the varied uses of language which was later developed by Wittgenstein.

W.P. Alston, furthermore, has mentioned the work of an another German philosopher Meinong, who began with this assumption, "…….every meaningful expression in a sentence (at least any meaningful expression that has the function of referring to something) must have a referent; otherwise, there would be nothing for it to mean. Hence, when we have an obviously meaningful expression that refers to nothing in the real world, for example, the Fountain of the Youth, in the sentence, 'De Soto was searching for the Fountains of Youth', we must suppose that it refers to a "subsistent" entity, which does not exist but has some other mode of being."[6] Indeed, this expression is based upon analysis. Thus, it is quite obvious that prior to Russell and Moore, many other philosophers were also analysts. In the opinion of A.J. Ayer, most of the philosophers who were really great, were analysts not metaphysicians. As he has said, "But I think it can be shown that the majority of those who are commonly supposed to have been great philosophers were primarily not metaphysicians but analysts."[7]

It reveals that analysis is not a new trend in the domain of philosophy. It begins with Greek Philosophy. However, there are some fundamental differences in the nature of analysis in the ancient and the contemporary approaches. On the one, the ancient philosophers were primarily metaphysicians whose chief aim was to acquire the knowledge of reality. They, therefore, conceived analysis as a means to acquire the knowledge of reality. Hence, analysis is not end in their philosophy. On the other, the contemporary philosophers are basically analysts. They accepted that to acquire the knowledge of reality is not the real job of philosophers. Actually, it is the job of scientists. The job of philosophers is to sheer analyse language. Hence, they eliminated metaphysics and assumed that metaphysical statement is nonsensical or meaningless. That is the major difference between the speculative philosophy and the analytical philosophy.

In the contemporary philosophy, the new trend of analytical philosophy developed into two different directions. On the one hand, there are some philosophers who observed that our ordinary language is vague, obscure and complex so that on the basis of it we can't solve the problems of philosophy. They, therefore, advocated the ideal language for solving the philosophical problems. On the other hand, there are some other philosophers who argued that our ordinary language is actually in order. Hence, its depth and most elaborated study is required to solve the problems of philosophy. They, therefore, argued that philosophical problems are not concerned with the meaning but these are concerned with the improper applications or uses of language. When, we use our language in proper contexts, there would be no problem. On this account, they shrugged off ideal language and argued in favour of ordinary language. Richard Rorty observed, "....... The view that philosophical problems are problems which may be solved (or dissolved) either by reforming language, or by understanding more about the language, we presently use."[8] Russell, Early Wittgenstein, Ayer and Carnap preferred for the first and led the foundation of ideal language philosophy. While, Later Wittgenstein, Austin, Strawson, Ryle and others preferred for the second and led the foundation of ordinary language philosophy.

The contemporary philosophers, like B. Russell and G.E. Moore were the founders of British Analytical Philosophy. In the real sense, the analytical philosophy began with Russell's theory of description. Russell assumes that our colloquial language or ordinary language is ambiguous, vague, and unclear. We, therefore, cannot distinguish between the logical and the grammatical form of ordinary language. For example, '*the author of Waverley is Scott*'. Here, there are two terms, *Scott* and *the author of Waverley*. Waverley is a name of a book written by Scott while, Scott is a name of a person. The question is: what is the meaning of *the author of Waverley*? If it is a name of Scott then *the author of Waverley* will be equivalent to Scott and therefore this sentence: the author of Waverley is Scott, will be a tautologous sentence. Tautologous sentence does not give any new information about the fact. While, in this sentence, we acquire some new information about Scott that he is the author of Waverley. Apart from this, if we accept that *the author of Waverley* is not the name of Scott, *viz.*, it is different from Scott and then the author of Waverley is Scott will be a contradictory sentence and thereby this sentence will be false. By virtue of this, Russell argued that the author of Waverley is not the proper name like Scott, but only a description of Scott. On this account, Russell distinguished between name and description. Name must indicate named, while description does not indicate any object. It seems that it also indicates an object but it doesn't indicate any object. By the process of analysis it can be lucidly shown. In this process, the term, the author of Waverley will not be used, in spite of this its meaning would be clear. Of course, such problem is created due to misunderstanding of the logical and the grammatical form. At the surface, it sounds like a simple sentence. However, as a ground reality this sentence is a complex sentence which has incorporated at least three simple sentences. For instance:

(1) At least one person who wrote Waverley.
(2) At most one person who wrote Waverley.
(3) Whoever wrote Waverley is Scott.

Russell conceived that by the process of analysis, it can be shown that its logical and grammatical forms are entirely different. By virtue of this, he brushed aside the ordinary language and advocated the ideal language. Ideal language contains merely symbols or simple sentences, which has certain logical form with certain meaning so that there is no ambiguity at the level of ideal language. Thus, while rejecting the ordinary language, Russell laid down the foundation of ideal language philosophy.

Russell by citing another example showed that there are some differences between the proper name and the description. For example, we may consider couple of sentences, like *the present king of France is bald* and *Napoleon is bold*. Albeit, the grammatical form of both of sentences is similar while, the logical form of these sentences is entirely different. *Napoleon* is the proper name in the second sentence; whereas, *the present king of France* is not the proper name in the first sentence. It is only a description, which describes about the present king of France. Indeed, at the level of ordinary language, we can't distinguish its logical and grammatical form.

Another analytical philosopher was G.E. Moore. In 1892, when Moore went to Cambridge, he was not interested in philosophy. So, he involved himself in the study of classics. Later, Russell diverted Moore from classics to philosophy. Moore, on the one hand, admitted this debt of Russell with full honesty in the following words: "I do not know that Russell has ever owed anything to me except mistakes, whereas, I have owed to his published works, ideas which were certainly not mistakes, and which I think very important."[9] Russell, on the other hand, claimed, "He took the lead in rebellion, and I followed, with a sense of emancipation."[10] These passages indicate the intimacy as well as regard of Russell and Moore for each other.

Moore is known notably on three counts. Firstly, prior to Moore, all philosophers believed that the function of philosophy was to solve the philosophical problems. Moore was the first philosopher, who changed this position and argued that the function of philosophy is not merely to give an answer to any philosophical problem, but it should clarify the concepts of these problems. Philosophical problems arise due to misunderstanding of the nature of question. If we clarify its concept, there would be no problem. While emphasizing this, Moore in his book *Principia Ethica* wrote, "It appears to me that in Ethics, as in all other philosophical studies, the difficulties and disagreements, of which its history is full, are mainly due to a very simple cause, namely the attempt to answer questions, without first discovering what question it is which you desire to answer."[11] Hence, he was not interested to initiate a new problem. He devoted himself to remove the vagueness and obscurity to those traditional problems, which the history of philosophy was full of. As he wrote, "I do not think that the world or the sciences would ever have suggested to me any philosophical problems. What has suggested problems to me is things which other philosophers have said about the world or about natural science."[12]

Generally, one understands that common sense is trivial for real knowledge. Moore shrugged off this fact and argued in favour of common sense knowledge. He, therefore, attempted to answer the questions raised by modern philosopher Emanuel Kant. Kant highlighted the question that if anyone doubts the existence of external world or 'things outside us', we can't give any satisfactory answer to it. Moore tried to answer this question in his article, *Proof of an External World*: "I can prove now, that two human hands exist. How? By holding up two hands, and saying, as I make a certain gesture with the right hand 'Here is one hand,' and adding, as I make a certain gesture with left hand 'and here is the other."[13]

Moore furthermore became more popular due to the method of analysis. Although analysis begins with Socrates but Moore was the first philosopher who based his whole theory on the method of analysis. By and large, there are two types of analysis, firstly, *the analysis of language* and secondly, *the analysis of concept*. In all likelihood, the term analysis has been used in the sense of linguistic analysis. Moore, however, used it in terms of analysis of concept. He conceived that we never analyse language, but only concept.

The question is: what does he mean by analysis? This is not an easy question to answer. Moore accepted that in the process of analysis, analysans and analysandum, both are similar in the concepts, but differ in the expressions. For instance, *a brother is a male sibling*. Here, there are two terms 'a brother' and 'a male sibling.' These two terms are conceptually identical but differ in expressions. Hence, a male sibling is a correct analysis of brother. Here, it is important to mention that in the process of analysis if both language as well as concept are similar, it would not be analysis at all. It must be fallacious. For instance, 'a brother is brother'. In this proposition, both concept as well as expression are similar. Hence, it is not real analysis and therefore, Russell called it *Paradox of Analysis*.

While emphasizing this, C.H. Langford in his article *Moore's Notions of Analysis*, wrote, "To give an analysis of a concept, Moore there suggests, is to discover some concept which is the same as the concept being analysed, but which can be expressed in a different way, by referring to concepts which were not explicitly mentioned in the expressions used to refer to the original concept."[14] Likewise, G.J. Warnock said, "It was always to consist in providing a verbal paraphrase of what was to be analysed, in the form of a longer, more explicit, but strictly synonymous phrase or sentence."[15] A.R. White also expressed the same attitude in his article *'G.E. Moore'*; "The expression used or the analysans must explicitly mention concepts which are not explicitly mentioned by the expression used for the analysandum."[16]

However, the weak point of Moore's analysis is that he could not distinguish between meaning and analysis and conceived that both are related with the concept. While, as a matter of fact, meaning is concerned with concept but analysis is not concerned with concept. It is concerned with language. Analysis means analysis of language. By virtue of this, Rudolf Metz commented upon Moore's analysis, "Moore was a good questioner but a bad answerer."[17]

Finally, Moore was the first philosopher, who advocated ordinary language for philosophical discussion. Indeed, Moore emphasised on common sense knowledge for philosophical discourse. Hence, it was natural that he preferred ordinary language for philosophical discourse. Ideal language and common sense knowledge are converse to each other to the extent that both are at the different levels. So, the philosopher who deals with common sense knowledge, naturally will operate with ordinary language. Thus, where most of the philosophers shrugged off ordinary language, Moore refuted the repudiations of ordinary language. As Norman Malcolm observed, "Moore's great historical role consists in the fact that he has been perhaps the first philosopher to sense that any philosophical statement which violates ordinary language is false, and consistently to defend ordinary language against its philosophical violators."[18]

Later, numerous distinguished philosophers like, L. Wittgenstein, P.F. Strawson, J.L. Austin, Gilbert Ryle, W.V.O. Quine and many others adopted ordinary language as their philosophical method. Of course, L. Wittgenstein was the first philosopher, who systematically developed this trend in his later work.

The tradition of analytical philosophy initiated and developed by Russell, attracted numerous distinguished philosophers of Cambridge and Oxford. Generally, it is believed that Wittgenstein brushed aside ordinary language and argued in the favour of ideal language, like Russell. This misconception begins with Russell's writing. It is well known that the introduction of Wittgenstein's book, *Tractatus-Logico-Philosophicus,* is written by Russell. In this introduction, he remarked that Wittgenstein repudiated ordinary language and replaced it by ideal language. As Russell observed, "In order to understand Mr. Wittgenstein's book, it is necessarily to realized what is the problem with which he is concerned. In the part of his theory which deals with symbolism, he is concerned with the conditions which would have to be fulfilled by a logically perfect language."[19] Likewise, John Wisdom and I.M. Copi have also substantiated Russell's contention. As Wisdom wrote, "Wittgenstein says that sentences picture facts. But hardly any sentences in ordinary language do picture facts. Wittgenstein does not wish to assert that they do. He is trying to point out an ideal to which some sentences try to attain."[20] Moreover, Copi stated, "The tendency to reject ordinary language seems to me to predominate. Wittgenstein was concerned with the construction of an adequate notion."[21]

Indeed, Wittgenstein criticised ordinary language in *Tractatus* on two counts:

- Firstly, in ordinary language, the same sign is used for varied purposes. For instance, 'is', term is used as a *copula,* as a *sign of equality,* as a *sign existence,* and the like.
- Secondly, two sentences which sound similar, differ in their logical form. For instance, *Napoleon is bald* and *the present king of France is bald.* Albeit, the grammatical form of both sentences is similar nonetheless their logical form is entirely different.

Indeed, our colloquial or ordinary language is obscure, vague, and complex. On this account, numerous problems arise in philosophy. Wittgenstein, therefore, argued, "All philosophy is the critique of language."[22] However, close in depth study of *Tractatus* reveals that Wittgenstein's aim was not to replace ordinary language by any symbolic or ideal language. As he himself remarked, "All propositions of our colloquial language are actually, just as they are, logically completely in order."[23] He simply wanted to remove its error, vagueness and complexity so that he used sign or symbolic language, whose form is perspicuous. The function of *sign language* or *ideal language* is not to replace *ordinary language* but to clarify the complexity and vagueness of ordinary language. He said, "Colloquial language is a part of the human organism and is not less complicated than it.

From it, is humanly impossible to gather immediately the logic of language. Language disguises the thought; so that from the external form of the clothes one can not infer the form of the thought they clothe, because the external form of the clothes is constructed with quite another object than to let the form of the body be recognised."[24]

Wittgenstein, therefore, advocated the ideal language, which elucidates the complexity of ordinary language. Bernstein wrote, "......for the purpose of this language is to show perspicuously what is 'hidden'."[25] On this account, W. Sellers[26] called it *'elucidatory language'* or *'ladder language'*. Hence, there is the least possibility of mistakes in ideal language. While describing the ideal language, Griffin said, "An ideal language is ideal, for Wittgenstein, because it makes clear features which are obscure in ordinary language, but the features that is being made clear, one should note, are the feature of ordinary language. The features, the essentials, are precisely what is common to both."[27]

Wittgenstein, therefore, accepted the process of analysis as suggested by Russell. In this process, ordinary language is divided into simple or elementary proposition which has very clear logical form. He further asserted that an elementary proposition cannot be divided into another elementary proposition. "One elementary proposition cannot be deduced from another."[28] It does not mean that it is ultimately undividable. It can be divided into *names* but not in another elementary proposition. He, therefore, argued that each elementary proposition is a systematic arrangement of names. "The elementary proposition consists of names. It is a connection, a concatenation, of names."[29]

The question is: "What does he mean by name?" Well, in his book *Tractatus*, Wittgenstein did not use the term 'name', in the ordinary sense. Generally, this word has been used for varied persons and things, like, Ram, Mohan, Himalaya, Ganga, and so forth. Wittgenstein did not use it in this sense. He holds that an ordinary name could be analysed into another form to the extent that it contains some specific characteristics which can be described. In that sense, name can't be simple. Whereas, Wittgenstein conceived 'name' as the simplest element of language which can be neither analysed into another form, nor can be defined by any other term. Wittgenstein called it a simple symbol or primitive sign. "The name cannot be analysed further by any definition. It is a primitive sign."[30] Thus, Wittgenstein did not give any example of name. This is the point, which differentiates the position of Wittgenstein from Russell. Russell gave some examples of name like *this* and *that*, which Wittgenstein did not conceive as names. According to Wittgenstein when we say *this* or *that*, it certainly insinuates something. And if a thing which indicates something that can't be simple. Moreover, he argued that although name is the simplest element of language, however, it is dead in itself.

Wittgenstein, furthermore, analysed the world. Indeed, world is complex so that it must be divided into another simple form which he called fact or state of affairs. "The world divides into facts."[31] The question is; what he means by state of affairs or fact? According to Wittgenstein, each atomic fact contains only object, *i.e.*, every atomic fact is the systematic arrangement of objects. "A state of affairs (a state of things) is a combination of objects."[32] The world is composed of such facts and can be completely analysed into them. "The world is the totality of facts not of things."[33]

Again, the question is; what is object? An object is the simplest element of the world but is unanalyzable into another form. Wittgenstein, therefore, didn't give any example of object. Apparently, he has not used the term object in simple sense, like any other object. For instance, wall, chair, table, pen, and so on and so forth. He has used this term in specific sense, which is the simplest element of the world.

Finally, Wittgenstein attempted to locate a real link between language and the world. He argued, "The name means the object. The object is its meaning."[34] It means that each name must represent an object and an object means that there is also a name. But it seems dead in itself. When will it be alive? It would be alive in an elementary proposition. An elementary proposition is the systematic arrangement of names. Hence, only an elementary proposition has sense and thereby it is meaningful. "Only propositions have sense; only in the nexus of a proposition does name have meaning."[35] Over and above, he conceived an object to be dead in itself. It would be alive in state of affairs or facts so that a state of affairs is systematic arrangement of objects. By virtue of this, Wittgenstein thought that every elementary proposition is the picture of an atomic fact, whereas, a fact is *what the case is* or *a state of affairs,* which makes a proposition true or false. For example, 'this pen is red'. This proposition indicates a state of affairs. If we experience a red pen corresponding to this state of affairs, the proposition will be true, otherwise false. Eventually, he holds that language is the systematic arrangements of elementary propositions. Likewise, the world is the systematic arrangements of facts. Hence, language is the picture of the world. However, both language and the world are complex, while names and object are dead. Hence, the only meaningful unites are atomic propositions in terms of language and atomic fact in terms of reality. In this way, Wittgenstein attempted to locate a real link between language and reality in the relation of atomic facts and atomic propositions. He conceived every elementary proposition as the picture of atomic fact. By virtue of this, every elementary proposition is meaningful. A proposition, which does not indicate any state of affairs, *i.e.*, atomic fact, is not proposition at all and therefore, it would be meaningless or nonsensical. Thus, metaphysical, ethical, theological and such type of other propositions which do not indicate any facts experienced, will be meaningless or nonsensical. Wittgenstein said, "The limits of my language are the limits of my world."[36] So, if anything is beyond of this world, we can't communicate it by our language. In such a situation, we should not say anything at all and therefore, we should maintain silence. "What can be said at all can be said clearly; and whereof one cannot speak thereof one must be silent."[37]

Over and above, Wittgenstein accepted that there are two types of propositions; tautologous and contradictory. These propositions tell nothing about facts yet these are not non-sensical or meaningless. The form of tautologous proposition is P or not P (P V ~ P) which is always true. In addition to the form of the contradictory proposition is P and not P (P ~ . P) which is always false. Although, these propositions tell nothing about facts, these are not nonsensical. Wittgenstein called them *senseless* inasmuch as these are concerned with the logical form of the world. "Tautologous and contradictory propositions are, however, not nonsensical, they belong to the symbolism in the same way that 'O' belongs to the symbolism of arithmetic."[38] Furthermore, "Tautology and contradiction are not pictures of reality. They exhibit no possible state of affairs. For the one allows every possible state of affairs, the other none."[39]

When Wittgenstein completed his celebrated book *Tractatus—Logico—Philosophicus,* he felt that all philosophical problems which are *indispensable*, have been finally solved. Later, numerous distinguished philosophers, F.P. Ramsey and Piero Sraffa were important among them, raised some questions. These criticisms gave a feedback for Wittgenstein to rethink all those issues which he has discussed in *Tractatus.* While describing the discussion with Ramsey, Wittgenstein said, "......Since beginning to occupy myself with philosophy again.........I have been forced to recognize grave mistakes in what I wrote in that first book (*i.e.*, the *Tractatus*). I was helped to realize these mistakes—to a degree with I myself am hardly able to estimate by the criticism which my ideas encountered from Frank Ramsey, with whom I discussed them in innumerable conversions during the last two years of his life."[40] Likewise, P. Sraffa's comment also compelled him to left his earlier formulations. Wittgenstein himself wrote, "...... his discussions with Sraffa made him feel like a tree from which all branches had been cut."[41]

Three criticisms against *Tractatus* were very important. "He came to reject in particular three of the implications or assumptions of his earlier views—first, that language is essentially used for one purpose, the stating of facts; second, that sentences essentially get their meanings in one way, namely through picturing; and third, that any language essentially has, though it may be hard to see it, the clear and firm structure of the formulae in a logical calculus."[42] Hence, Wittgenstein again pondered over these mistakes and attempted to eliminate them in his later formulations, which was posthumously compiled under the title of *Philosophical Investigations* in 1953.

In the meantime, a group of some other contemporary philosophers like Moritz Schlick, Otto Neurath, Rudolf Carnap, Herbert Feigle, Fredrick Waismann, Victor Craft including a number of Scientists and Mathematicians like, Hans Hann, Philip Frank, and Kurt Gödel, initiated a philosophical movement. This movement was initiated in 1922 at Vienna, under the leadership of Moritz Schlick, and more systematically developed in 1929, when an International Conference was organized for shaping the objectives of this movement in *Prague*. In this year, a journal, *'The Scientific World View: The Vienna Circle'* was published by this group of philosophers. In 1930, Carnap and Reichenbach who were from Germany, published a journal, with the title; *Erkenntnis*. Later on, they published a series of books under the title of *Unified Science*. In 1933, a British philosopher A.J. Ayer also associated himself with this movement.

This movement was popularly known as *Vienna-Circle* or *Logical Positivism* or *Logical Empiricism* or *Scientific Empiricism*. It has contained the empiricism of Hume, the positivism of Comte and Mach, along with the logical analysis of Frege, Moore, Russell and Early Wittgenstein. Logical positivism was indeed the modified form of the earlier empiricism of Hume. However, there are some fundamental differences between Hume and logical positivists:

- Hume's empiricism is concerned with the analysis of ideas while logical positivist's analysis is concerned with the analysis of language.
- Hume's analysis is psychological whereas logical positivist's analysis is logical.
- Hume's conceived that metaphysics is impossible while logical positivists accept that metaphysics is non-sensical.

Later, this movement was developed and propagated by a number of other philosophers like A.J. Ayer at Oxford, Hans Reichenbach at Berlin and E. Negal and C.W. Morris at America. Meanwhile, a founder member of this movement, Moritz Schlick was killed by his student in 1936. In 1934, Hans Hann died. In addition, other philosophers like Rudolf Carnap, Feigle, and others, transferred their activities in American Universities from Vienna due to political vicissitudes. Likewise, Otto Neurath moved for Holland and Waismann to England. Thus, this movement was scattered. Merely, Otto Neurath attempted to survive it at the international level and initiated editing of a philosophical journal *The International Encyclopedia of Unified Science*, which was the modified name of the earlier journal *Erkenntnis*.

The objectives of this movement were fundamentally two; firstly, the *elimination of metaphysics* and secondly, *the demonstration of science*. The question is: what is meant by metaphysics? This is controversial question. Logical positivists, however, relate metaphysics with supernatural being, like God. As A.J. Ayer wrote, "The fundamental postulate of metaphysics is that there is a super—(or hinter—) phenomenal reality ....... It is the aim of metaphysics to describe a reality lying beyond experience and therefore any proposition which would be verified by empirical observation is *ipso facto* not metaphysical."[43]

Prior to the logical positivists, there were some other philosophers like, Comte, Hume, and Kant who also argued against metaphysics. However, the method which was followed by logical positivists was entirely different and is known as the *theory of meaning*, or *the verification theory of meaning*. This theory advocates that the meaning of a proposition rests upon the method of its verification. If the meaning of a proposition hinges upon the method for its verification then if a proposition is verified by different ways, naturally its meaning would be varied. The issue remains what would be the appropriate criterion to decide the meaning of a proposition? This controversy arose even in the *Vienna Circle*. Hence, positivists changed their position and conceived that firstly, verification meant verification by sense experience. And secondly, they conceived *verification* as a criterion but not as a method deciding the meaning of a proposition. Hence, if a proposition is verified by sense experience, would be meaningful otherwise it would be non-sensical. As Gilbert Ryle said, "But, roughly stated, it lays down that the meaning of a statement is determined by the way in which it can be verified, where its being verified consists in its being tested by empirical observations."[44] Likewise, G.J. Warnock argued, ".....the meaning of any statement is shown by the way in which it could be verified—it is being assumed that verification must always at least terminate in empirical observation, or sense-experience."[45] Accordingly, only those propositions are significant which can be verified by sense experience and all those propositions which can't be verified by sense experience are meaningless or non-sensical.

The question is: if verification means verification in sense experience then all those propositions which are not verified in experience, would be non-sensical. In that sense, all historical propositions, like, 'Babar was the founder of Mughal Empire' and all such universal propositions, like 'if anything would be thrown above, it will come back on the earth', must be non-sensical. Even all mathematical and logical propositions would be meaningless inasmuch as these are not verifiable by sense experience. However, one may say that although these propositions are not verifiable by sense experience, instead these are not meaningless.

By virtue of this, logical positivists divided language into two sorts—Emotive and Cognitive. Emotive statements express feelings, passions, emotions etc., while, the cognitive statements express the cognitive and literal meaning of a sentence. They further divided cognitive statement into two sorts; analytic and synthetic. An analytical proposition is that whose truth underpins over the symbols of its proposition while a synthetic proposition is that whose truth is decided by sense experience. While distinguishing between the analytic and synthetic proposition, A.J. Ayer said, "........a proposition is analytic when its validity depends solely on the definitions of the symbols it contains, and synthetic when its validity is determined by the facts of experience."[46] Only these two sorts of propositions are meaningful and all those propositions which are beyond this category, are meaningless or non-sensical. Hence, metaphysical, ethical, religious, aesthetic propositions are nonsensical to the extent that these propositions are neither analytical nor synthetic. As Ayer wrote, "And as tautologies and empirical hypotheses form the entire class of significant propositions, we are justified in concluding that all metaphysical assertions are nonsensical."[47]

D.M. Dutt comments that in the sense of elimination of metaphysics, logical positivists are more radical *vis-à-vis* earlier positivists like Hume. "...... while earlier positivists objected to metaphysical speculation either because it is unprofitable or because its truths cannot be proved, the new positivists object to it because logical analysis of metaphysical language convinces them that all metaphysical propositions are meaningless. The anti-metaphysical positivism is, therefore, more radical."[48] Thus, logical positivists demonstrate the meaninglessness of metaphysics and bestows a secure ground of sciences. Only scientific propositions are meaningful which are verified by experience. However, they used the term *scientific* in the wide sense which contains all sorts of empirical propositions.

Numerous criticisms were raised by some distinguished philosophers against this theory so that while distinguishing varied sorts of verification theory, A.J. Ayer endeavoured to prove the meaninglessness of metaphysical proposition. These verification principles are as follows:

- Practical and Principle verification
- Strong and Weak verification
- Direct and Indirect verification

Several criticisms were also raised by some distinguished philosophers like Lazerowitz, Sir I. Berlin, John Passmore, B. Russell, L. Wittgenstein, G.J. Warnock, E.E. Harris and so on. Our present goal is not to discuss the details of these principles along with its criticisms. However, it is quite obvious that logical positivists failed to establish their objectives. These verification methods are either so wide which prove the existence of both scientific as well as metaphysical propositions or they become so narrow that even scientific propositions become non-verifiable.

Here it is important to mention that Hume also proved the impossibility of the existence of God to the extent that he is the beyond of our experience. "If we take in our hand any volume of divinity or school of metaphysics, for instance; let us ask, Does it contain any abstract reasoning concerning quantity or number? No, does it contain any experimental reasoning concerning matter of fact and experience? No, commit it then into the flames: for it can contain nothing, but sophistry and illusion."[49] While commenting upon Hume's contention, John Passmore wrote, "........throw metaphysics into the fire, and science goes with it, preserve science from flames and metaphysics come creeping back."[50] Eventually, in 1960, in a Television broadcast, A.J. Ayer claimed that now logical positivism is dead. Indeed, it speaks of the honesty of logical positivists.

After the publication of the celebrated book *Tractatus-Logico Philosophicus* (1922), Wittgenstein kept himself away from philosophy till 1929. He thought that all the philosophical problems which are indispensible have been finally solved. While describing the temporary withdrawal of Wittgenstein, John Passmore wrote, "In his years of silence, however, he was not left entirely alone. Ramsey and Braithwaite sought him out in his Austrian retreat and, for some part of the time, he was in close contact with Schlick and Waismann. Round about 1928, his interest in philosophy revived. The stimulus may have been Brower's lectures on the foundation of mathematics, the set of problems, which had originally led Wittgenstein to philosophy. In 1929, he returned to Cambridge."[51]

In 1929, Wittgenstein again returned back to philosophy and gradually attempted to rectify those mistakes which were raised against *Tractatus,* firstly, by his lectures and then by some written materials which were delivered in his lectures, known as *The Blue Book* and *The Brown Book.* There were a few typed copies of these which were circulated among his private students and admirers. Posthumously, his work was published under the title of *Philosophical Investigations* (1953). Although, both books (*Tractatus* and *Investigations*) dealt with the same problems, the contents and positions propounded, provided entirely different answers. Wittgenstein asserted about his work: "It travels over a wide field of thought criss-cross in every direction: it is full of unanswered questions, unamplified hints, imaginary dialogues, images, metaphors, and epigrams."[52] In his investigations, Wittgenstein refuted many theories of *Tractatus* and laid a foundation of *ordinary language philosophy*.

In the *Tractatus,* Wittgenstein accepted that the meaning of every simple proposition is clear and definite. Now, he thinks it was a prejudice. "The man who is philosophically puzzled sees a law in the way a word is used, and trying to apply this law consistently, comes up against cases where it leads to paradoxical results."[53]

"We want to say that there can't be any vagueness in logic. The idea now absorbs us that the ideal 'must' be found in reality."[54]

"When we believe that we must find that order, must find the ideal, in our actual language, we become dissatisfied with what we ordinarily called 'propositions', 'words', 'signs'."[55]

In *Tractatus,* Wittgenstein accepted that the meaning means an object and the object is its meaning, *i.e.*, the meaning of a word is that object, which it refers to. But now he asserts: firstly, the meaning of words does not consist of objects. For example, if the meaning of 'Ram' is Ram (as a person who exists in actual world), then after the death of 'Ram' this word 'Ram' will be nonsensical. But it is not correct. Wittgenstein himself admitted that it would be appropriate to say that 'Ram died' but it will be wrong to say that the meaning of Ram has died. While emphasizing this, John Passmore argued, "The meaning of slab, then, does not consist in the objects it names, but in the way it is used in a language. If the actual slab—the physical object—were part of the meaning of slab, Wittgenstein argues, we ought to be able to say things like: 'I broke part of the meaning of the word slab', 'I laid a hundred parts of the meaning of the word slab today.' Such sentences are obvious nonsense........"[56] Secondly, there are numerous words, which do not indicate any objects like *But, And, Perhaps* and so on. It reveals that the meaning is not an object. "For a large class of cases—though not for all in which, we employ the word meaning it can be defined thus: the meaning of a word is its use in the language."[57]

In *Tractatus,* he claimed, 'meaning is a mental activity.' Later, he asserted that if it was correct, then we utter 'ABC', and its meaning should be 'pen is red.' Obviously, it is not practically possible. Thus, he argued, "And nothing is more wrong-headed than calling meaning is a mental activity."[58]

In *Tractatus,* Wittgenstein holds that there are certain or definite meaning of the word. On the basis of the certainty of meaning, he propounded his popular theory known as *picture theory.* This theory advocates that language is the picture of reality. He, therefore, locate a real link between language and reality. Now, he conceives that there is no certain meaning. The meaning of a word rests upon its use. A word or sentence is used in varied contexts and therefore, it acquires varied meanings. As Wittgenstein wrote, "But how many kinds of sentences are there? Say assertion, questions, and command. There are countless kinds: countless different kinds of use of what we call symbols, words/sentences. And this multiplicity is not something, fixed, given once for all; but new types of language, new *language-games,* as we may say, come into existence and others become obsolete and get forgotten. (We can get a rough picture of this form the changes in Mathematics). Here the term *language-game* is meant to bring into prominence the fact that speaking of language is part of an activity, or of a form of life.

Review the multiplicity of language-games in the following examples, and in others:

"Giving orders, and obeying them—
Describing the appearance of an object, or giving its measurements—
Constructing an object from a description (a drawing)—
Reporting an event—
Speculating about an event—
Forming and testing a hypothesis—
Presenting the results of an experiment in tables and diagrams—
Making up a story and reading it—
Play—acting—
Singing catches—
Guessing riddles—
Making a joke; telling it—
Solving a problem in practical arithmetic—
Translating from one language into another—
Asking, thanking, cursing, greeting, praying."[59]

Wittgenstein, therefore, attempted to prove that language works like a game. The word *game* is used for various types of games, like Board games, Card games, Outdoor games, Indoor games and so forth. There may not be one common characteristics involved in each game. Only some similarities may be found common in all games. Wittgenstein called it as *family resemblance*. For instance, a family does not contain only one common feature related to all family members. Indeed, they have different characteristics. However, there are some common properties found in two or more than two but not all. On this account, we call them a family member. The same conditions apply even in the realm of language. It facilitates that there are no certain meaning of a word or sentence. A word or sentence is used in varied contexts and acquires varied meanings. Only use or context decides the 'meaning' of a word or a sentence. In his words "I shall also call the whole, consisting of language and the actions into which it is woven, the language-games."[60] Furthermore, "One can't guess how a word functions. One has to look at its use and learn from that."[61] Moreover, "Every sign by itself seems dead. What gives it life?—In use it is alive, life breathed into it there?—or is the use its life?"[62]

Wittgenstein conceded that if we use words in their proper context in everyday life, there will be no problem. Problems arise when we don't use our words without considering its actual context. "Philosophical problem has the form: I don't know my way about."[63] So, he emphasised, "What is your aim in philosophy?—To show the fly the way out of the fly—bottle."[64] Apart from, "For the clarity that we are aiming at is indeed complete clarity. But this simply means that the philosophical problems should completely disappear."[65] He further holds that philosophical problems are just like mental disease or intellectual perplexity. The function of philosophy is, therefore, not to set forth any philosophical doctrine, but to cure deep disquietudes. "The cure lies in bringing words back from their metaphysical to their everyday use."[66] "Philosophy is a battle against the bewitchment of our intelligence by means of language."[67] The prime causes of philosophical disease is one-side-diet, the nourishing of thinking with only one kind of example. For instance, the word *knowledge*. By and large, knowledge is conceived as a perceptual knowledge. Here is the philosopher's puzzle. How the knowledge of past and future would be possible? In addition, the term *knowledge* is also used in varied sense. Keith Lehrer[68] showed that this term has been broadly used in three senses; firstly, in sense of *competency* which is concerned with 'How'; secondly, in sense of *acquaintance* which is concerned with 'Whom'; and thirdly, in sense of *information* which is bound up with 'What is'. The problems arise, when we use this term without knowing its contexts. If we use our words in their proper context, there would be no problem at all. "For philosophical problems arise, when language goes on holiday."[69] Furthermore, "The confusions which occupy us arise when language is like an engine idling, not when it is doing work."[70]

Warnock synthesizes this contention and said, "We have to resist 'the bewitchment of our intelligence by means of language', superstitions 'produced by grammatical illusions', 'through a misinterpretation of our forms of language'; therefore, we must look 'into the working of our language, and that in such way as to make us recognize those workings: in spite of an urge to misunderstand them'. We must make it our aim to 'command a clear view', in spite of the fact that 'our forms of expression prevent us in all sorts of ways' from seeing clearly what lies before us."[71]

While commenting upon this D.M. Dutt wrote, "This is turning of thinker back to practice as the cure for the disease of idle speculation—which would remind us of Hume who also says that practice is the cure for scepticism. Yet the irony is that both Hume and Wittgenstein spent their lives in speculation rather than action. And a careful studying of the *investigations* would show that its author is not always describing grammatically the uses of problem words, but often trying to ascertain the meaning of words and validity of theories in the light of empirical facts and contingencies as well, stepping freely beyond the domain of language."[72]

Although, Moore was the first philosopher who initiated ordinary language for philosophical discourse, the real credit, however, goes to Wittgenstein, who systematically developed it after 1929 at Cambridge. As P.F. Strawson admitted, "Right or wrong, Wittgenstein's particular doctrines are of the greatest interest and importance. But the value of the book as a model of philosophical method is greater still (Here I do not refer to idiosyncrasies of style and form). It will consolidate the philosophical revolution for which, more than anyone else, its author was responsible."[73] Similarly, A.M. Quinton emphasised, "British Philosophy in the last forty years would have been a very different, and poorer thing if Wittgenstein had taken his own prohibitions literally."[74] I would also like to add a quote from V.C. Chappell, "……. Wittgenstein converted large numbers of philosophers to the view that philosophy is essentially linguistic. It is in large part owing to his work that this view is dominant in Anglo-American Philosophy today."[75]

Later on, ordinary language philosophy moved into two different directions; some followed Wittgenstein and others modified his theory. A group of philosophers like, John Wisdom, F. Waismann, G.E.M. Anscombe, Norman Malcolm and M. Lazerowitz, were directly impressed by the later work of Wittgenstein so that they developed this approach at Cambridge and known as *Cambridge school's of ordinary language philosophy*. Whereas, some other philosophers mostly of Oxford, like, P.F. Strawson, G. Ryle, J.L. Austin, H.L.A. Hart, Sir Stuart Hampshire, R.M. Hare, J.O. Urmson, G.J. Warnock and others, modified the ordinary language philosophy of Wittgenstein and developed it at Oxford after the Second World War. This tradition is known as *Oxford school's of ordinary language philosophy*. John Passmore asserted, "At Oxford, Wittgenstein's ideas entered a very different philosophical atmosphere from that which prevailed at Cambridge.... At Oxford, then, Wittgenstein's ideas were grafted on to an Aristotelian philosophical stock; the stock has influenced the resultant fruits, which, among other things, are considerably drier and cooler than their Cambridge counterparts."[76] The following summaries the contributions of analytical philosophy:

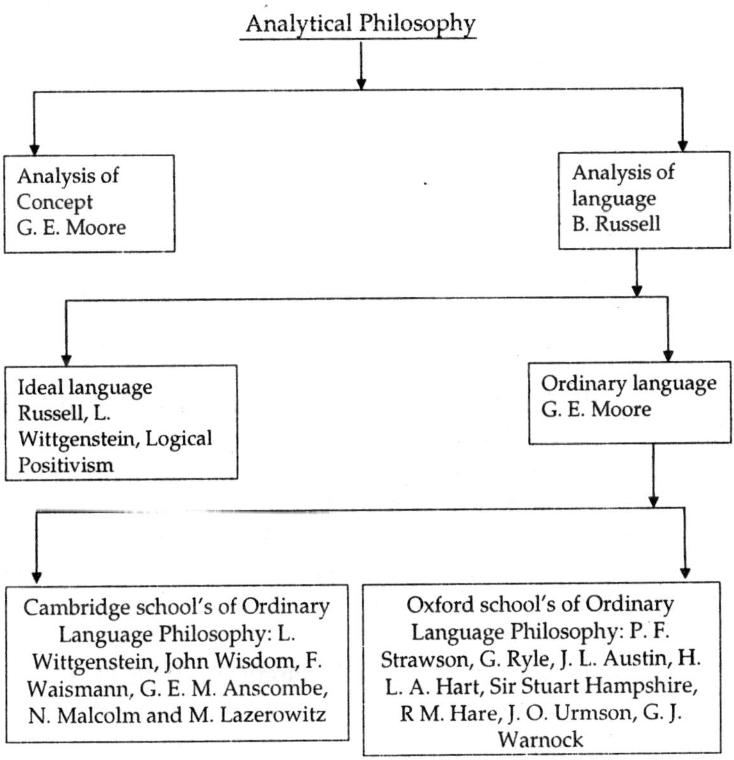

In the course of time Oxford became the main centre of ordinary language philosophy. The contributions of Oxford philosophers on ordinary language philosophy were so prominent that many considered this approach and Oxford as synonymous. While describing this, A.M. Quinton wrote, "Oxford has undoubtedly been the centre of British philosophical activity since the War. It has regained the position it had in the late nineteenth century in the epoch of Green and Bradley, which it lost to Cambridge soon after the turn of the century with the start of the philosophical careers of Russell and Moore and which Cambridge kept until the retirement of Wittgenstein in 1947. There is nothing surprising about this. If anything is odd it is that Oxford should have lost its commanding place."[77]

The question is: did ordinary language philosophers agree on some common factors? Well, the school of ordinary language philosophy was not a movement or a programme like, logical positivism, pragmatism and so forth. The philosophers of this discipline adopted different styles. It is, therefore, difficult to identify some common factors in all ordinary language philosophers. However, our effort is to show some similarities as *family resemblance.*

The philosophers of the ordinary language schools (Cambridge as well as Oxford) agreed with Wittgenstein on basically three factors. Firstly, all philosophers are against the ideal language and thereby they conceded that ordinary language is actually in order. Secondly, all of them conceived that philosophical problems are concerned with the improper uses of language, *i.e.*, problems arise when we do not understand the actual uses of language. As Quinton wrote, "They believed the proper method of criticism to be a demonstration, by careful attention the ordinary uses of words, that these metaphysical propositions both embodied and rested upon misusage of language."[78] Thirdly, they also agreed that the metaphysics of ancient style are nonsensical. It does not mean that they are anti-metaphysician in terms of logical positivism. Their chief aim was to study the *uses* along with its *nuance distinctions* of ordinary language but not to eliminate metaphysics. By virtue of this, they ignored metaphysics and endeavoured to solve the real philosophical problems. As Warnock observed, "For one thing, although philosophy at present is for the most part admittedly *unmetaphysical,* it is not doctrinally *anti-metaphysical* in the manner of logical positivism; ........"[79]

There were some significant differences between both of the schools. Firstly, on the one, Wittgenstein and other Cambridge philosophers began their philosophical interest with the study of some specific problems. The Oxford philosophers, on the other, were interested to solve general problems of philosophy. For instance, G. Ryle in his book, *The Concept of Mind* endeavoured to elucidate the logical structure of mental concepts and on the basis of the uses of words and sentences he attempted to solve the problem of mind-body relationship, raised by Descartes. Likewise, P.F. Strawson also discussed the concept of *person,* in his book *Individual.* V.C. Chappell said, "Comparisons are hard, but it may be said in general that the Oxford philosophers tend to be more interested in the actual details of ordinary language and in drawing general philosophical conclusions than the Wittgensteinians, who tend to restrict themselves to the solution of specific problems."[80]

Secondly, Wittgenstein admitted that philosophical problems arise due to improper uses of words or sentences. So, these problems are not like real problem but these are like, *mental disease* or *intellectual perplexity.* The aim of philosophy is, therefore, therapeutic. Lazerowitz stated, "Its function is wholly therapeutic. Like Freudian analysis, to which it is often compared, it dissolves illusions and restores to health."[81] Oxford philosophers, however, conceived that some problems may be like therapeutic but not all problems are like therapeutic. Hence, the role of Philosophy is not only negative but also constructive. Quinton wrote, ".....Ryle and Austin agreed in rejecting Wittgenstein's idea of philosophy as a therapeutic undertaking aimed at the relief of intellectual perplexity. They regarded these puzzles more as incitements to the systematic task of establishing the informal logic of the ordinary use of expressions or, as Ryle also described it, of mapping the logical geography of concepts."[82] Ryle, in his article *Rayaumont Colloquium,* admitted, "As far as the differences and similarities between Ryle and the later Wittgenstein go, I think that the essential difference is this: I come from a medical background, where I picked up the habit of distinguishing sharply between diseases, which make you sick, and other states of health, which do not. Wittgenstein talks as if philosophical problems were symptoms of a sickness of which the patient must be cured. I think, for myself, that not finding these problems troublesome would be a sign of remarkable stupidity. Therefore, I use a language, which is, so to speak, less clinical than Wittgenstein's, and I less inclined than he to practice surgery. In part of that reason, and in part of others, I have no compunction about saying that some of the things which philosophers have said are true, and that others are false. The latter, to be sure, are the vast majority."[83] Likewise, Austin suggested that the systematic and scientific study of ordinary language is important in itself and therefore he called it *linguistic phenomenology* or *expanded science of grammar*.

Thirdly, Wittgenstein believed that the function of philosophy is only to describe the actual uses of language. Hence, he didn't provide any theoretical ground for the systematic study of ordinary language philosophy. As he wrote, "Philosophy may in no way interfere with the actual use of language, it can in the end only describe it."[84] While, Oxford philosophers advocated on certain background for acceptance of ordinary language as a philosophical method. They conceived that the study of ordinary language is important in itself to the extent that there are numerous nuance distinctions involved in it which we can't understand carelessly. The study of ordinary language in the totality is, therefore, indispensable for solving the philosophical problems. While emphasizing this, Broyman stated, "Connected with this is the insight that ordinary language is the medium in which human activities take place first and most of all. It is in ordinary language that I make friends and enemies, plan my future, influence others, make commitments, receive assurances. And novel, unheard of phenomena become intelligible and can be dealt with when they left their native surroundings or jargon and entered the realm of ordinary language (or perhaps when ordinary language has extended itself and embraced them)."[85] Austin, moreover, remarked, ".......our common stock of words embodied all the distinctions men have found worth drawing, and the connexions they have found worth marking, in the lifetimes of many generations: these surely are likely to be more numerous, more sound, since they have stood up to the long test of the survival of the fittest, and more subtle, at least in all ordinary and reasonably practical matters, than any that you or I are likely to think up in our arm-chairs of an afternoon—the most favoured alternative method."[86] Likewise, J.O. Urmson also asserted, "If one asks these (ordinary language) philosophers what such minute description is good for, and why they attempt so close a study of the nuances of ordinary language, they will answer, first of all, that they consider it interesting in itself and useful for discovering the conceptual resources of our language. They will add that one thereby gains a better understanding of the world to which these concepts are applied."[87]

Fourthly, some philosophers of Oxford school attempted to clarify some specific concepts which they considered useful for their philosophical methods and more so for philosophy. For instance, P.F. Strawson tried to clarify the concept of *person*, while G. Ryle attempted to clarify *category* as well as the nature of *use* in ordinary language. Similarly, Austin also attempted to elucidate enormous definable words in his varied articles. Wittgenstein, however, did not pay attention to these issues.

The position of Oxford school's of ordinary language philosophers can be placed as a mid-way between two opposite disciplines represented by Later Wittgenstein and logical positivists. On the one hand, they advocate ordinary language, like, Later Wittgenstein. They also believe, on the other hand, in logical properties and its relations of varied forms of discourse like, logical positivists. While emphasizing this, A.M. Quinton wrote, "In general terms, then, the method of

Oxford philosophers lay somewhere in between the professed method of Wittgenstein and the methods of the logical positivists of the 1930s. With the positivists and against Wittgenstein they believed that the job of philosophy was to set out the logical properties and relations of the various forms of discourse in a systematic way. But with Wittgenstein and against positivists they rejected the ideal of linguistic perfection suggested by formal logic, concerning themselves with the description of language as it actually is rather than with the extrication of some ideal essence from it or with the proposal of a logically superior conceptual system as an alternative to it."[88]

The above discourse highlights the position of British analytical philosophy. It also discusses the positions of both *Oxford school of ordinary language philosophy* as well as *Cambridge school of ordinary language philosophy* and shows that there is clear cut difference between both of the schools. In the forthcoming chapter, we shall discuss the position of J.L. Austin who was one of the eminent scholars of Oxford school of ordinary language philosophy.

## REFERENCES

1. Urmson, J.O. (1956). *Philosophical Analysis*, p. (vii).
2. Quinton, A.M. (1964). Contemporary British Philosophy. In D.J.O. Connor (Ed.), *A Critical History of Western Philosophy*, p. 531.
3. Plato, Republic, Book X, 596. In W.P. Alston (1964) (Quoted). *Philosophy of Language*, p. 1.
4. Aristotle, Metaphysics, Book Zeta, Chapter 1. In W.P. Alston (1964) (Quoted), *Philosophy of Language*, p. 2.
5. Berkeley, G. (1710). "Treatise Concerning the Principles of Human Knowledge." In I.M. Copy and Cohen Carl (Quoted) *Introduction to Logic* (1994), p. 80.
6. Alston, W.P. (1964). *Philosophy of Language*, p. 2.
7. Ayer A.J. (1958). *Language Truth and Language*, p. 52.
8. Rorty, Richard (1970). *Introduction to the Linguistic turn*, p. 3.
9. Passmore, J. (Quoted) (1984). *A Hundred Years of Philosophy*, p. 201.
10. *Ibid.*, p. 201.
11. *Ibid.*, p. 206.
12. *Ibid.*, p. 201.

13. *Ibid.*, p. 211.
14. *Ibid.*, p. 201.
15. Warnock, G.J. (1959). *English Philosophy Since 1900*, p. 27.
16. White, A.R. (1964). G.E. Moore. In D.J.O. Conner (Ed.), *A Critical History of Western Philosophy*, p. 467.
17. Quoted from Passmore, J. (1984). *A Hundred Years of Philosophy*, p. 206.
18. Malcolm, N. (1964). Moore and Ordinary Language. In V.C. Chappell (Ed.), *Ordinary Language Philosophy*, p. 23.
19. Wittgenstein, L. (1961): *Tractatus-Logico-Philosophicus.* Translated by D.F. Pears and B.F. McGuiness, T. 5.5563.
20. *Ibid.* p. 7.
21. Wisdom, John (1931): *Logical Construction, Mind*, p. 202.
22. Wittgenstein, L. (1961): *Tractatus-Logico-Philosophicus.* Translated by D.F. Pears and B.F. McGuiness, T. 4.0031.
23. Copi, I.M. (1958): *Objects Properties and Relations in Tractatus, Mind*, p. 146.
24. Wittgenstein, L. (1961): *Tractatus-Logico-Philosophicus.* Translated by D.F. Pears and B.F. McGuiness, T. 4.002
25. Bernstein, R.J. (1961): *Wittgenstein's Three Languages.* p. 283.
26. Sellers, W. (1962): *Naming and saying, Philosophy of Science*, pp. 7-26.
27. Griffin, James. (....): *Wittgenstein's Logical Atomism*, p. 140.
28. Wittgenstein, L. (1961): *Tractatus-Logico-Philosophicus.* Translated by D.F. Pears and B.F. McGuiness, T. 5.134.
29. *Ibid.* T. 4.22
30. *Ibid.* T. 3.26.
31. *Ibid.* T. 1.13
32. *Ibid.* T. 3.02
33. *Ibid.* T. 1.1
34. *Ibid.* 3.203
35. *Ibid.* T. 3.3
36. *Ibid.* 5.6.
37. *Ibid.* T. 7.
38. *Ibid.* T. 4.4611.
39. *Ibid.* T. 4.462.
40. Von Write, G.H. *Biographical Sketch*, reprinted in Malcolm, Memoir, p. 16. Quoted from D.N. Diwedi (1977): *A Study of Wittgenstein's Philosophy*, pp. 131-32
41. *Ibid.* p. 132.
42. Warnock, G.J. (1959). *English Philosophy Since 1900*, p. 67.
43. Ayer, A.J. (1934). *Demonstration of the Impossibility of Metaphysics* printed in Mind, July 1934.
44. Ryle, G. (Ed.). (1956). *Revolution in Philosophy*, p. 74.
45. Warnock, G.J. (1959). *English Philosophy Since 1900*, p. 45.

46. Ayer, A.J. (1958). *Language Truth and Logic*, p. 78.
47. *Ibid.*, p. 41.
48. Dutt, D.M. (1970). *The Chief Currents of Contemporary Philosophy*, p. 465.
49. Shankar, S.G (........): Hume's Enquiry Concerning Human Understanding. In *Philosophy in Britain Today* (Ed.), pp. 154-55.
50. Passmore, J. (1966). *A Hundred years of Philosophy*, p. 390.
51. *Ibid.* p. 424.
52. Warnock, G.J. (1959). *English Philosophy Since 1900*, p. 63.
53. Wittgenstein, L. (1958). *The Blue and Brown Books*, p. 27.
54. Wittgenstein, L., (1953) *Philosophical Investigations*, p. 109.
55. *Ibid.*, p. 105.
56. Passmore, J. (1966). *A Hundred years of Philosophy*, p. 428.
57. Wittgenstein, L. (1953). *Philosophical Investigations*, p. 43.
58. *Ibid.*, p. 693.
59. *Ibid.*, p. 23.
60. *Ibid.*, p. 7.
61. *Ibid.*, p. 340.
62. *Ibid.*, p. 432.
63. *Ibid.*, p. 123.
64. *Ibid.*, p. 309.
65. *Ibid.*, p. 133.
66. *Ibid.*, p. 116.
67. *Ibid.*, p. 109.
68. Lehrer, Keith. (1971): *Knowledge*, p. 1.
69. Wittgenstein, L. (1953). *Philosophical Investigations*, p. 38.
70. *Ibid.*, p. 109.
71. Warnock, G.J. (1989): J.L. Austin, p. 3.
72. Dutt, D.M. (1970). *The Chief Current of Contemporary Philosophy*, p. 485.
73. Strawson, P.F. (1956). Review of Philosophical Investigations. In George Pitcher (Ed.), *Wittgenstein*, p. 64.
74. Quinton, A.M. (1964). Contemporary British Philosophy. In D.J.O. Connor (Ed.), *A Critical History of Western Philosophy*, pp. 540-41.
75. Chappell, V.C. (1964). *Ordinary Language: Contemporary Perspectives in Philosophy Series*, pp. 1-2.
76. Passmore, J. (1984). *A Hundred years of Philosophy*, pp. 440-41.
77. Quinton, A.M. (1964). Contemporary British Philosophy. In D.J.O. Connor (Ed.), *A Critical History of Western Philosophy*, pp. 545-46.
78. Quinton, A.M. (1964). Contemporary British Philosophy. In D.J.O. Connor (Ed.), *A Critical History of Western Philosophy*, p. 546.
79. Warnock, G.J. (1959). *English Philosophy Since 1900*, p. 160.
80. Chappell, V.C. (1964). *Ordinary Language: Contemporary Perspectives in Philosophy Series*, p. 3.

81. Lazerowitz, M. (1977). The Philosophy of Language: Freud and Wittgenstein. In Gerld Runkle (Ed.), *Theory and Practice An Introduction to Philosophy*, p. 566.
82. Quinton, A.M. (1964). Contemporary British Philosophy. In D.J.O. Connor (Ed.), *A Critical History of Western Philosophy*, p. 546.
83. Ryle, G. (1961). Royaumond Colloquium. In Rorty Richard (Ed.), *Introduction in the Linguistic Turn*, p. 305.
84. Wittgenstein, L. (1953). *Philosophical Investigations*, p. 124.
85. Broyman. A. (1974). *The Philosophy of Language: Historical Foundations and Contemporary Issues*, p. 118.
86. Austin, J.L. (1979). A Plea for Excuses. In Warnock and Urmson (Eds.), *Philosophical Papers*, p. 182.
87. Urmson, J.O. (1970). The History of Philosophical Analysis. In Rorty Richard (Ed.), *Introduction to the Linguistic turn*, p. 300.
88. Quinton, A.M. (1964). Contemporary British Philosophy. In D.J.O. Connor (Ed.), *A Critical History of Western Philosophy*, p. 546.

2

# J.L. Austin: Aims and Method

John Langshaw Austin born in Lancaster, U.K. on 26th March 1911, did not live long. He passed away prematurely in February 1960. He is considered as one of the most eminent personalities in the domain of ordinary language philosophy. His ability was conspicuously outstanding. He was not only a genius by birth but also a hard worker and a strict disciplinarian in his job. He was a natural leader. His leading position among the philosophers was not only limited in Oxford where he lived and taught but also it extended to Britain and more so in the whole philosophical world.

Austin did not publish any book in his lifetime. He published only seven papers. His first paper was *Are There A Priori Concepts?*, published in 1939. These seven papers along with three other unpublished papers were compiled by G.J. Warnock and J.O. Urmson under the title of *Philosophical Papers* in 1961. Later, in the second edition (1970), the same editors incorporated two other unpublished papers. In the third edition (1979), one additional paper reconstructed by J.O. Urmson from Austin's notes, was also included. Austin's unpublished work was posthumously presented in two other books *Sense and Sensibilia* and *How to Do Things with Words*. The first, *Sense and Sensibilia* (1962) was compiled by G.J. Warnock, hinges upon the theory of perception. The second, *How to Do Things with Words* (1962) was compiled by J.O. Urmson and Marina Sbisa based on speech act theory, which was delivered by Austin under William James Lecture Series at Harvard University in 1955. The second revised edition of *How to Do Things with Words* was published in 1975 by J.O. Urmson and Marina Sbisa. Later, P.H. Nidditch added a new index in it in 1980. The three books are classics in the realm of analytical philosophy. In addition, Austin edited *W.H.B. Joseph's Lectures on the Philosophy of Leibniz* (1949) and translated Frege's *Grundlagen der Arithmetik* (1950).

D.S. Colman, a Queen's Fellow, teaching at Shrewsbury described Austin's joining as a scholar in his institution in 1924: "Austin was already an accurate and sensitive scholar, particularly in Greek—'for above the usual level even of an able Sixth Form'; and if in character and temperament he was then (as indeed he was always) quite without eccentricity, appearing even to be 'a reasonably typical Salopian of the period', it could already be foreseen that he would achieve real academic distinction. As a House Monitor his authority, which he did not hesitate to exercise, was unquestioned, as was also the strict sense of justice by which it was directed; his juniors found him a little remote, but by no means ineffectual; and in any case they were (Paul Dehn reports) proud of him."[1]

He duly justified his award when he was selected for a scholarship at Balliol in 1929. In 1931, when he was still a young learner, he won the Gaisford Prize for Greek Prose. At Balliol, he was greatly impressed by his tutor C.G. Stone, the author of *The Social Contract of the Universe*. In 1933, he got first class in Greats and was selected to a Fellowship at All Souls. He had not decided to choose a philosophical career till now. Later, fascinated by philosophy, he finally decided to adopt it as his career. According to Austin, "... philosophy was an excellent training for young men; there was no better way of making them rational—in those days his highest term of praise—if only because it generated in them a critical, indeed a skeptical attitude, the only antidote, in his view, to what he called being chuckleheaded."[2]

It may be mentioned that later two distinguished Philosophers B. Russell and Prichard, stimulated and encouraged Austin to opt philosophy as a career. He was attracted to Russell because he deemed him genius, openminded and endowed with the highest logical capacity, essentials to establishment philosophical doctrines. He considered Prichard a rigorous and minute thinker. Albeit, Austin never countenanced with Prichard's contention, instead he had a lot of regard, praise, and admiration for Prichard. Austin conferred with Prichard twice by letter. Firstly, when he was facing some problems in Aristotle's Ethics and secondly, when he was analysing the term *Promising*. While highlighting this G.J. Warnock wrote, "This last had long been a particular preoccupation of Prichard's; and his concern may well have contributed to the genesis of Austin's long and patient investigation of performative utterances."[3] Likewise, Sir Isaiah Berlin remarked, "His own doctrine of performative function of words seem to me to owe a good deal to Prichard's painful self-questionings about, for example, the logical character of promises……"[4]

In 1935, he became a tutor and Fellow at Magdalene and then he regularly began to teach Philosophy. In 1939, when the second world war started, Austin also participated in the war approximately for six years. In 1940, he was commissioned by Intelligence Crops and posted to the war office in London. A.J. Beattie, who served with Austin, said, "…… his superiors in rank very quickly learned that he was an outstanding authority on all branches of intelligence work, and they soon depended on his advice for more than would normally have been considered proper in any headquarters."[5] He performed outstanding duty of his career during the war period. Eventually, with the rank of lieutenant colonel and the O.B.E., he returned from unquestioned war service and again joined the academic institution. Later on, he was posted in university administration, where he was characteristically remembered for great care over detail. In 1952, he was elected the White's Professor of Moral Philosophy. He had not published any book till that day. G.J. Warnock wrote, "He had been elected in 1952 to one of Oxford's only three (at that time) professorships of philosophy—a noteworthy election, in that the chair in question, that of the White's Professor of Moral Philosophy, was 'officially' in a field in which he was only pretty marginally interested and had published nothing; it must have been felt that it would nevertheless have looked obviously wrong to elect anybody else, and fortunately the University had long countenanced considerable latitude in such matters."[6]

When Austin returned from excellent war service, his philosophical interest and activity had entirely changed. Initially when he became a Fellow and Tutor of Magdalen, his philosophical interest was in the traditional philosophers like, Plato, Aristotle, Leibniz, Kant and so forth. He persistently read Aristotle's *Nicomachean Ethics* and also delivered lectures on this topic. He was also fascinated with Plato particularly the *Theatetus* as well as with the *Kantian Philosophy*. Once he delivered lectures on Leibniz's philosophy in the Philosophical Society. He also delivered lectures on Plato and Aristotle after post war period, but in a different way. It does not reveal that in the post war spell, he altered his philosophical method. Warnock observed that two things have been unchangeable; firstly, nuance and the most elaborated study of *ordinary language* and secondly, *co-operative pursuit* for philosophical discourse. "This Austin had long believed, and always did believe; but he had formed, I think, since before the war two new views about philosophical procedure. The first and most notorious of these was that 'ordinary language' should not only, in the interests of clarity and common understanding, usually the employed by philosophers; it should also be, thoroughly and in detail, studied by them. ........the other view, which has been rarely discussed largely because, I believe, it has never been taken seriously, may be guessed to have arisen directly from his war experience: it was that philosophy could be, and should be, a co-operative pursuit."[7] Eventually, he settled with contemporary philosophical problems and kept the traditional problems in the background.

Apart from, Austin initiated a meeting, known as *Saturday Morning*. This was a weekly meeting, lasting from two to three hours. Austin was the pioneering philosopher to pursue discourse on philosophy in this meeting. Numerous distinguished philosophers used to participate and confer about the recent and pertinent problems of philosophy. "....... these meetings were a pilot project for, or perhaps merely the closest practicable approximation to, the kind of systematic collaboration that Austin had in mind...... Very often the topic for a term's discussion would be the critical examination of some currently fashionable semi-technical term—the term 'disposition', for example, or 'symbol', or 'class'; for a time mathematical logic came under scrutiny; sometimes a text would be discussed—Frege's *Grundlagen*, Aristotle's *Ethics*, Wittgenstein's *Philosophical Investigations*, and (in the term before Austin's death) Chomsky's *Syntactic Structures*."[8]

Never satisfied with existing philosophical doctrines, Austin was at the pace of highest intellectual ambition and therefore he criticized even those doctrines which were popular among the contemporary philosophers. Sir I. Berlin has acknowledged that Austin used to hold a regular philosophical discussion. Berlin, therefore, invited many distinguished Oxford philosophers like, A.J. Ayer, MacNabb and Woozley, for this discussion. In addition, other participants were Stuart Hampshire and Donald Mackinnon who were Fellows of All Souls. Numerous recent topics were discussed. Four of these important topics were: *theory of perception; a priori truth; verification principle;* and *personal theory and knowledge of other minds*. Austin forcefully criticized all these theories. He criticized even A.J. Ayer's theory of perception and then Ayer exclaimed: "You are like a greyhound, who doesn't want to run himself, and bites the other greyhounds, so that they can't run either."[9]

Austin was invited to deliver the William James Lectures Series at Harvard University in 1955. At that time, George Pitcher, a graduate student at Harvard discussed with Austin on a topic of Wittgenstein's *Philosophical Investigations* which was a popular subject among philosophers at that time. Pitcher said, "I had maintained that a word or sentence is a universal, namely, a certain aspect of the structure of the sounds that are made in uttering it or of the marks that are made in writing it. From this it apparently follows that if a person utters the appropriate sounds, he must necessarily be saying the relevant word or sentence. Austin demonstrated the falsity of this view with a simple example. Suppose I ask you 'If cold water is iced water, what is cold ink?' and you reply 'Iced ink.' You would have uttered the sounds 'I stink', but not the words 'I stink'; rather in saying the words 'Iced ink', you uttered the sounds 'I stink'."[10] Pitcher, therefore, observed that Austin had an outstanding critical mind.

An important question arises as to what was the philosophical method of Austin? Albeit, Austin never articulated his method in a systematic way, nonetheless, whatever he has expressed in his varied articles, especially in *A Plea for Excuses, Ifs and Cans* and *Three ways of spilling Ink,* something is very clear. Firstly, Austin conceived that this method is not *sine qua non* for everyone who attempts to study any philosophical theory. He, however, himself comprehended it so valuable and so interesting that he could not deem about other methods. Over and above, Austin assumed that this method is not entirely new, numerous distinguished philosophers from Socrates to Moore had already practiced it in their diverse formulations.

This method underpins over the careful observation of ordinary language. The pervasive and systematic study of ordinary language is important in itself to the extent that there are enormous nuance distinctions involved in ordinary language which we can't comprehend by sitting on an easy armchair. We should, therefore, consider all facets of ordinary language very carefully without any prejudice and then one should apply it in appropriate contexts. Austin too believed, like Wittgenstein and other ordinary language philosophers that all these philosophical problems arise due to improper uses of language. Ordinary language is, however, not as easy as one understands it. Indeed, it contains numerous salient characteristics which we can't understand carelessly. As Austin said, "First, words are our tools, and, as a minimum, we should use clean tools: we should know what we mean and what we do not, and we must forearm ourselves against the traps that language sets us. Secondly, words are not (except in their own little corner) facts or things: we need therefore to praise them off the world, to hold them apart from and against it, so that we can realize their inadequacies and arbitrariness, and can relook at the world without blinkers. Thirdly, and more hopefully, our common stock of words embodies all the distinctions men have found worth drawing, and the connexions they have found worth marking, in the lifetimes of many generations; these surely are likely to be more numerous, more sound, since they have stood up to the long test of the survival of the fittest, and more subtle, at least in all ordinary and reasonably practical matters, than any that you or I are likely to think up in our arm-chairs of an afternoon—the most favoured alternative method."[11]

While describing Austin's method, J.O. Urmson wrote, "First, he claimed, it was only common prudence for anyone embarking on any kind of philosophical investigation, even one that might eventually involve the creation of a special technical vocabulary, to begin with an examination of the resources of the terminology already at his disposal; clarification of ordinary language was thus the 'begin-all', if not the 'end-all', of any philosophical investigation. Second, he thought that the institution of language was in itself of sufficient interest to make it worthy of the closest study. Third, he believed that in general a clear insight into the many subtle distinctions that are enshrined in ordinary language and have survived in a lengthy struggle for existence with competing distinctions could hardly fail to be also an insight into important distinctions to be observed in the world around us—distinctions of an interest unlikely to be shared by any we might think upon our unaided initiative in our professional arm-chairs."[12]

Later, Austin's method was commented upon by some philosophers on certain grounds. Firstly, although Austin criticized the use of technical terminology in philosophy, instead he himself used enormous technical terms. Here, it is important to mention that Austin never brushed aside the uses of technical terms. He, however, argued that numerous terms are coined and used in hasty without deep thinking. This approach is not sound for philosophy. Secondly, it is said that Austin conceived ordinary language as sacrosanct. This criticism is also not correct. Austin did not believe that ordinary language is sacrosanct. He always endeavoured to modify and improve it and thereby he proclaimed that one should always remember that ordinary language is not the last word but it is only the first word. "Certainly ordinary language has no claim to be the last word, if there is such a thing. It embodies, indeed, something better than the metaphysics of the Stone Age, namely, as was said, the inherited experience and acumen of many generations of men.......Certainly, then, ordinary language is not the last word: in principle it can everywhere be supplemented and improved upon and superseded. Only remember, it is the first word."[13]

Austin advocated ordinary language for philosophical discourse. This method contains notably two things: firstly, it requires *minimum justification* inasmuch as it is simply concerned with the use and meaning of the words. In this regard, we should always remember Austin's warning that *what we should say when and what we should mean by it.* "....... why it is an attractive subject methodologically, at least if we are to proceed from 'ordinary language', that is, by examining what we should say when, and so why and what we should mean by it. Perhaps this method, at least as one philosophical method, scarcely requires justification........"[14] Secondly, when we examine what we should say when, we may not pay attention only on the uses or meanings but also its relation to the realities or world in which these words have been used. Hence, the systematic and scientific study of ordinary language is very important in itself. On this account, Austin called it *Linguistic Phenomenology*. While articulating his position, he wrote in his article *A Plea For Excuses:* "When we examine what we should say when, what words we should use in what situations, we are looking again not merely at words (or 'meanings', whether they may be) but also at the realities we use the words to talk about: we are using a sharpened awareness of words to sharpen our perception of, though not at the final arbiter of, the phenomena. For this reason I think it might be better to use, for this way of doing philosophy, some less misleading name than those given above—for instance, linguistic phenomenology......."[15]

Some other distinguished philosophers have also used the term *phenomenology* but in different way. Immanuel Kant, an eminent German philosopher, for instance, has used the term Phenomena and Noumena. Noumena is concerned with transcendental world and is based upon faith, while phenomena is bound up with physical world and underpins over sense experience. Likewise, another contemporary German Philosopher Edmund Husserl also used this term as a philosophical method and underpinned over his whole philosophy on the study of phenomenological method. He conceived phenomenology as an enterprise to remove blinkers and re-look the thing as they are. Husserl's phenomenology is, however, related with the study of consciousness and its concerning objects, *i.e.*, the whole actual and possible world along with even God. While describing this, Cerf wrote, ".........acts of the transcendental subject constitute the whole sphere of objects, including myself, the essences, God, the actual world, and possible worlds as well as the existence or non-existence of all of these. Husserl assigned to phenomenology the study of these constitutive acts and their interconnections; and he believed that this study should and could be as rigorous a science as, say, geometry."[16] Husserl's phenomenology is, therefore, naturally concerned with the transcendental world to the extent that this can only be realized by intuition. On this account, it is known as *esoteric phenomenology*.

Here it is important to mention that Husserl did not conceive consciousness as a pure-consciousness which is beyond of all sorts of dualism. He assumed that mere consciousness without object is impossible inasmuch as consciousness is a relative term which has two poles; *noema* and *noesis*. In this regard, the nature of consciousness in Husserl's philosophy is different and Śaṅkar's philosophy. Āchārya Śaṅkar believed in pure-consciousness which is without relation to any object, while Husserl believed in that consciousness which is always relative to its inherent objects.

Husserl's phenomenology attracted some other young German philosophers, like Heidegger. Heidegger also began his journey with this slogan that to *re-look the world without blinkers*, like Husserl. But he reached different conclusion and threw the Husserl's esoteric phenomenology in the garbage pail. Hence, both are similar only in the method but they are different in their achievements. On the one hand, Husserl's phenomenology is concerned with the study of phenomena, Heidegger's phenomenology, on the other hand, is concerned with the discovery of Being, so that it is not limited with phenomenal world. He attempts to find out a foundation of the phenomena. By virtue of this, he emphasises on experience rather than intuition, unlike Husserl. Moreover, Husserl's phenomenology is related with the study of consciousness and its whole sphere of objects, while Heidegger's phenomenology is related with the study of man's being in the world. As Cerf said, "This blinkers Heidegger discovered in Husserl were in the main the nexus of traditional concepts supposedly grasping man's being in the world: man as subject or consciousness relating himself through acts to objects the totality of which is the world."[17]

Plainly, Husserl's phenomenology ended up with the transcendental world, while, Heidegger's phenomenology related with the actual world and known as *mundane phenomenology*. Hence, there is the sharp difference between esoteric phenomenology and mundane phenomenology. "Clearly, there is an enormous difference within mundane phenomenology between the esoteric, radically idealistic, methodically self-conscious work of its founder and the popular phenomenology of many of his followers who were commonsensically realistic in epistemology, satisfied with blinkerlessness of vision and honestly of description as method, and, as to their subject, preferred this world to all possible words."[18]

Austin's position is in the mid-way between the esoteric and the mundane phenomenology. Austin accepted that we can't solve the philosophical problems in terms of inherited experience inasmuch as there are so many mistakes involved in the ordinary language. So, we should use our words very carefully. As Austin observed, "......superstition and error and fantasy of all kinds do become incorporated in ordinary language and even sometimes stand up to the survival test."[19] When Austin assumed that what we should say when, he plainly accepted that we should not use our words in hasty or in respect of inherited experience. We should use our words without blinkers or prejudices. Austin, however, used this project in the domain of philosophy of language and asserted that the *total speech act must be seen in the total speech situations*. Thus, Husserl and Austin both began their journey with this projection that we should re-look at things, without blinkers. Husserl applied this enterprise in the realm of metaphysics. Austin, however, used it in the sphere of philosophy of language and called it *linguistic phenomenology*. Walter Cerf said, "Here is one point of resemblance between Austin and Husserl himself. Husserl's transcendental doctrine stands and falls with the concept of acts performed by consciousness; Austin made 'performance of act' the concept serving as genus in the doctrine of speech acts. The point of this resemblance, however, is not any similarity between Austin's and Husserl's doctrine….."[20]

Austin never accepted Husserl's esoteric phenomenology. In this sense, Austin's linguistic phenomenology is similar to mundane phenomenology or popular descriptive phenomenology which never goes beyond this actual world. However, there are inherent weakness of this phenomenology, like "lack of methodological and logical rigour, subjectivism, unsystematic activity……"[21] In this regard, Austin's linguistic phenomenology is more systematic and logical *inter alia* mundane phenomenology. According to Cerf, linguistic phenomenology is a formal mode, while, mundane phenomenology is a material mode. He, however, conceived that in Austin's phenomenology this distinction is fused. When Austin holds that the *total speech act must be seen in the total speech situations* then indeed he sees a relation between language and reality. It is not purely a linguistic analysis. "Looking at the total speech act in the total speech situation is quite different from looking at language in the way the Wittgensteinians used to. Language has become part of a whole nexus of transactions between man and world. To relook at this whole dimensions of language may be called phenomenology; but it may hardly be called phenomenology in formal mode, not even in the most informally formal mode."[22]

An eminent philosopher C.W.K. Mundle, denounced Austin's linguistic phenomenology. According to him, Austin's phenomenology has no novelty. Whatever Austin assumed, we have been already practicing from the beginning of our childhood. Austin, in his whole enterprises, merely emphasized on the *word-use* and thereby he has said nothing about the *realities* in which we use our words. Mundle, moreover, suggested to Austin that it would be better if Austin uttered *what we do say* or *what people would say*, in the place of *what we should say when*. As Mundle said, "But the method by which Austin seeks to sharpen our perception of things is reminding ourselves of the familiar ways in which we do, normally, describe them, of the everyday uses of English that we learnt as children." This seems to be one of the least promising ways of sharpening, or indeed altering, our perception of anything. Austin did introduce new descriptions, like performative utterance, stipulate if and illocutionary forces; but these were descriptions of word-uses and not of 'the realities we use words to talk about.' What Austin sharpened our perception of is grammar.

Notice an ambiguity in Austin's wording: "What we should say when. If he had written what we do say or what people would say, it would have been clear that his linguistic inquiries were intended to be empirical, descriptive. In asking what we should say, the 'should' may be taken as an 'ought', and the answers may be prescriptive, corrective. Indeed, Austin not infrequently makes statements about English usage which could not be justified by appealing to dictionaries or to everyday talk."[23]

The other important theme about Austin's philosophy is that he disowned *idiosyncratic view* and emphasised on his unique method, *co-operative pursuit*. In all likelihood, in arts or even in sciences, intellectuals emphasised on individual pursuits or contributions or single-minded handling of work. Austin brushed aside this method and argued in favour of *co-operative pursuit*. He has always used this method not only in Oxford, where he was a tutor and fellow but also in the war period. In the spell of the war, only the patient and systematic collaboration had solved numerous difficulties and strenuous problems. Austin argued that philosophical problems are comparably wrangle, vast, obscure and perplexing *vis-à-vis* the other problems. So why not apply this method in the sphere of philosophy or other social sciences? He plainly assumed that if your aim is real and serious you cannot achieve it only by individual efforts. "I owe it to the subject to say, that it has long afforded me what philosophy is so often thought, and made, barren of—the fun of discovery, the pleasures of the co-operation, and the satisfaction of reaching agreement."[24] Similarly, G.J. Warnock remarked, "If anything, was his view of philosophical method: discussion—careful, critical discussion—in the hope and with the intention of reaching agreement, and with the consequential hope of getting something right."[25]

Austin suggested that firstly, a philosopher or a group of philosophers should select a specific field for their discourse. In all likelihood, it should be based upon their interest. By and large, the field of the discourse should be related to great philosophical issues and then they should develop to concepts and vocabulary related to this pertinent issue. The philosophers should proceed firstly, by thinking and then by looking for synonyms, and synonyms of synonyms not only by consulting dictionaries but also by consulting even non-philosophical literature. Again, they should examine all these data to determine whether these are legitimately appropriate or not. We should further attempt to detect those sentences in which these words have been used. Moreover, at the second phase we should make up a story regarding the uses of these words and also to examine what other philosophers and grammarians have said regarding these issues. Eventually, they should find a *consensus* among open-minded philosophers. While emphasizing this, Keith Graham remarks, "In concrete terms, such a procedure has three phases. In the first, we are to make as complete a collection as possible of all the linguistic items, expressions, idioms, etc., which are relevant to the particular area of thoughts we are concerned with. For this Austin recommends working through dictionary and any other appropriate literature..... We would then turn to other useful sources, such as law books, which will contain details of various types of pleas in mitigation, and psychology books, which will contain various interesting classifications of different types of behaviour."[26]

Graham further elaborates, "......the second phase consists in breathing life into them. This we do by imagining, in as precise and detailed a way as possible, different situations and attempting to reach an agreement on what we should say when they obtained. In this way, we attempt to differentiate between idioms and expressions by reference to the different situations to which they are allocated. As well as discussions about what we should say when, this second phase also sometimes involves decisions about when we should say what. That is, sometimes we begin by specifying a situation and then determine which a number of possible expressions is appropriate to it, but at other times we begin by selecting the expression and then working back to a specification of the kind of situation in which the expression would be appropriate."[27]

The final stage is elaborated by Graham, "..... if we can reach agreement in this second phase then we have acquired some data which we may go on to explain in the third phase. Such an explanation will consists in 'an account of the meaning of these expressions, which we shall hope to reach by using such methods as of Agreement and Difference; what is in fact present in the cases where we do use, say, deliberately, and what is absent when don't."[28]

Austin conceived this method as empirical and scientific and argued that it would be healthy for scientific inquiry. He predicted that with the collaboration of philosophers, grammarians and the students of language of a new science, *science of language* would emerge and thereby it would be a separate discipline from philosophy of language. Austin believed that it would not be an entirely new thing in the history of philosophy to the extent that so many disciplines like mathematics and psychology have been separated from philosophy from time to time in the past. In all likelihood, a new discipline, *science of language* would be separated from philosophy in the future. "In the history of human inquiry, philosophy has the place of the initial central sun, seminal and tumultuous: from time to time it throws off some portion of itself to take station as a science, a planet, cool and well regulated, progressing steadily towards a distant final state. This happened long ago at the birth of mathematics, and again at the birth of physics: only in the last century we have witnessed the same process once again, slow and at the time almost imperceptible, in the birth of the science of mathematical logic, through the joint labours of philosophers and mathematicians.

Is it not possible that the next century may see the birth, through the joint labours of philosophers, grammarians and numerous other students of language, of a true and comprehensive Science of Language? Then we shall have rid ourselves of one more part of philosophy (there will still be plenty left) in the only way we ever can get rid of philosophy, by kicking it upstairs."[29]

The above discussion delineates Austin's aims and method in brief. It also focuses on certain issues which were pertinent for young philosophers. One of the important things of Austin's method is that he emphasised on *co-operative pursuit* for philosophical discourse and therefore, he brushed aside idiosyncratic method. Indeed, only with concerted and conscientious effort, we may able to cope with the wrangle and obscure problems of philosophy. When we share our ideas with our colleagues or other disciplinarians, it gives a feedback to correct ourselves. Such feedback would necessarily be advantageous not only for a person but also for our society and more so for whole human being. The above discussion gives us an idea of Austin's method of philosophizing. In the chapters that follow we shall discuss the important aspects of his philosophy of language.

## REFERENCES

1. Warnock, G.J. (1969): *J.L. Austin: A Biographical Sketch*. In K.T. Fann (Ed.), Symposium on J.L. Austin, pp. 3-4.
2. Berlin, Sir, I. (1973): *Austin and the Early Beginnings of Oxford Philosophy*. In Berlin and others (Eds.) Essays on J.L. Austin, p. 1.
3. Warnock, G.J. (1969): *J.L. Austin: A Biographical Sketch*. In K.T. Fann (Ed.). Symposium on J.L. Austin, p. 4.
4. Berlin, Sir, I. (1973): *Austin and the Early Beginnings of Oxford Philosophy*. In Berlin and others (Eds.), Essays on J.L. Austin, p. 2.
5. Warnock, G.J. (1969): *J.L. Austin: A Biographical Sketch*. In K.T. Fann (Ed.), Symposium on J.L. Austin, p. 8.
6. Warnock, G.J. (1969): *J.L. Austin* p. 1.
7. Warnock, G.J. (1969): *J.L. Austin: A Biographical Sketch*. In K.T. Fann (Ed.) Symposium on J.L. Austin, p. 12.
8. *Ibid.* pp. 14-15.
9. Berlin, Sir, I. (1973): *Austin and the Early Beginnings of Oxford Philosophy*. In Berlin and others (Eds.), Essays on J.L. Austin, p. 10.

10. Pitcher, G. (1973): *Austin: A Personal Memoir*. In Berlin and others (Ed.), Essays on J.L. Austin, p. 23.
11. Austin, J.L. (1979): *A Plea for Excuses*. In G.J. Warnock and J.O. Urmson (Eds.), Philosophical Papers, pp. 181-82.
12. Urmson, J.O. (1969): *Austin's Philosophy*. In K.T. Fann (Ed.), Symposium on J.L. Austin, p. 23.
13. Austin, J.L. (1979): *A Plea for Excuses*. In G.J. Warnock and J.O. Urmson (Eds.), Philosophical Papers, p. 185.
14. *Ibid.*, p. 181.
15. *Ibid.* p. 182.
16. Cerf, Walter, (1969): *Critical Review of How to Do Things with Words*. In K.T. Fann (Ed.), Symposium on J.L. Austin, pp. 374-75.
17. *Ibid.*, pp. 376.
18. *Ibid.* pp. 375-76.
19. Austin, J.L. (1979): *A Plea for Excuses*. In G.J. Warnock and J.O. Urmson (Eds.), Philosophical Papers, p. 185.
20. Cerf, Walter, (1969): *Critical Review of How to Do Things with Words*. In K.T. Fann (Ed.). Symposium on J.L. Austin, p. 376.
21. *Ibid.* p. 376.
22. *Ibid.* p. 378.
23. Mundle, C.W.K. (1979): *A Critique of Linguistic Philosophy*, p. 86.
24. Austin, J.L. (1979): *A Plea for Excuses*. In G.J. Warnock and J.O. Urmson (Eds.), Philosophical Papers, p. 175.
25. Warnock, G.J. (1969): *J.L. Austin: A Biographical Sketch*. In K.T. Fann (Ed.), Symposium on J.L. Austin, p. 10.
26. Graham, K. (1977): *J.L. Austin: A Critique of Ordinary Language Philosophy*, pp. 32-33.
27. *Ibid.*, pp. 32-33.
28. *Ibid.*, p. 33.
29. Austin, J.L. (1979): *Ifs and Cans*. In J.O. Urmson and G.J. Warnock (Eds.), Philosophical Papers, p. 232.

3

# Performative and Constative Utterances

At the outset of his celebrated book *How to Do Things with Words*, Austin made a clear cut distinction between the constative and the performative utterance. The constative utterances are those utterances which always describe some fact or state something so that these are concerned with *saying* something. The performative utterances are those which are always used to perform some act rather than to describe or state some fact and therefore these are concerned with *doing* something. He, however, himself observed some problems in this distinction. He, therefore, brushed aside this distinction and argued that *every speech is an act*. In other words, an utterance not only describes some fact but also performs some act, *viz.*, each utterance has two poles; *saying* as well as *doing*. This doctrine is known as speech act theory.

By and large, philosophers conceived that each meaningful statement has only one function, *viz.*, to describe some fact or to give some information about fact. If a statement doesn't describe or inform something, it is meaningless or non-sensical. This position was basically taken by logical positivists. Later on, L. Wittgenstein, altered this position in his later formulations and he argued that language has not only one function, *i.e.*, to describe or inform something. This is indeed one important function of language but not all functions of language. In spite of describing or informing something, it has so many other functions, like greeting, thanking, stimulating, commanding, and so forth. This position of Wittgenstein is deemed as revolutionary in the domain of analytical philosophy which led the foundation of a new school known as *ordinary language philosophy*.

J.L. Austin too accepted the position of Wittgenstein that there are varied uses of language. It will be, therefore, wrong to say that language has only one job, namely to describe some fact or describe some state of affairs, and he called it a *descriptive fallacy*. Logical positivists argued that the meaningful statements are either *synthetic* which describes some fact or *analytic* which is concerned with formal truths like, Mathematics and Logic. And all those statements which are neither analytic nor synthetic are nonsensical. While commenting upon this distinction, Austin said, "We very often also use utterances in ways beyond the scope at least of traditional grammar. It has come to be seen that many specially perplexing words embedded in apparently descriptive statements do not serve to indicate some specially odd additional feature in the reality reported, but to indicate (not to report) the circumstances in which the statement is made or reservations to which it is subject or the way in which it is to be taken and the like. To overlook these possibilities in the way once common is called the *descriptive fallacy*; ...........Not all true or false statements are descriptions and for this reason I prefer to use the word *constative*. Along these lines, it has by now been shown piecemeal, or at least made to look likely, that many traditional philosophical perplexities have arisen through a mistake—the mistake of taking as straightforward statements of fact utterances which are either (in interesting non-grammatical ways) nonsensical or else intended as something quite different."[1]

Austin distinguished statement into two types: the constative and the performative. The constative utterance always describe some facts or state some facts, so that it is always either true or false. If there is a fact in accordance with the utterance, the utterance will be true otherwise false. While there are some other utterances, which are superficially similar in structure with the constative utterances, but they are neither nonsensical from the grammatical point of view, nor are true or false from factual point of view. These utterances have always been used to do something *vis-à-vis* to say something. In addition to this, these utterances are always in the form of *felicitous* or *infelicitous inter alia* true or false. If an act is performed in accordance with our utterance, the utterance will be felicitous otherwise infelicitous. Austin called it performative utterance. As he stated, ".......statements, which are not nonsense and which contain none of those verbal danger signals which philosophers have by now detected or think they have detected (curious words like 'good' or 'all', suspect auxiliaries like 'ought' or 'can', and dubious constructions like the hypothetical): all will have, as it happens, humdrum verbs in the first person singular present indicative active. Utterances can be found, satisfying these conditions, yet such that:

- They do not describe or report or constate anything at all, are not true or false; and
- The uttering of the sentence is, or is a part of, the doing of an action, which again would not normally be described as, or as just, saying something."[2]

Precisely, performative utterances do not describe any fact but always stimulate to do something to the hearer or address. While emphasizing the characteristics of performative utterance, G.J. Warnock wrote, "The utterances to be first investigated exhibit three features in particular—the first, their form is that of impeccably correct, quite ordinary indicative sentences, containing no curious words and in no problematic construction—sentences which, in fact, look grammatically just like statements: but second, they do not actually state (Austin uses the term constate) anything at all, and are not true or false: and third, the uttering of such sentences is, or is a part of doing something—something, further, which would not normally or naturally be described as (just) saying something. It is the third feature, of course, which accounts for their being called performatives."[3]

Austin was the first philosopher in the history of philosophy, who strongly propounded the doctrine that there may be some utterances which sound like statement but as a ground reality these are fundamentally different from the statement. They always perform some act and therefore Austin called them *performatives*. This was a revolutionary steps in the realm of ordinary language philosophy. In the view of Walter Cerf, "In fact, performatives became Austin's hallmark as the ghost in the machine had become Ryle's and language games Wittgenstein's."[4]

R.M. Chisholm, however, argued that it would be wrong to say that there are some utterances which always perform something *vis-à-vis* to say or describe something. Each utterance is, therefore, in both the forms performative as well as descriptive. Hence, it would be inconsistent to say that an utterance is non-descriptive and called it *performative fallacy*. As he wrote, "To suppose that the performance of the latter non-descriptive function is inconsistence with a simultaneous performance of the former, descriptive function, might be called an example of the *performative fallacy*."[5]

In this regard, Austin attempted to distinguish between the constative and the performative utterances. Firstly, the constative is used to say something or state something, whereas, performative is used to do something. Secondly, if the performatives fail to achieve their goal, they will not be false like constative but will be unhappy. While, if it will succeed in their jobs, they will not be true, but merely happy. The former is, therefore, true or false while the later is happy or unhappy. Thirdly, the constative is moved towards *word to word*, while the performative is moved towards *word to world*.

While distinguishing between the constative and the performative utterances, Keith Graham wrote, "The initial characterisation of performatives is partly negative, in that it rests on a contrast between them and constatives and the claim that, unlike constatives, they are not true or false. At one point Austin suggests a way of further developing this characterisation by way of contrast with constatives:

(a) In the case of constative utterance, *e.g.* 'he is running', it is some independently existing fact, separate from the utterance, which makes the utterance true.

(b) In the case of a performative utterance, *e.g.* "I apologise", it is the happiness of my utterance, which makes it a fact that I apologise.

In other words, it is suggested that performatives and constatives exhibit a difference in 'direction of fit' with the world. It is how the worlds is which determines how he assesses a constative in its appropriate dimension, *viz.*, truth and falsity; whereas it is our assessment of a performative in its dimension of happiness and unhappiness which determines how the world is."[6]

Now the question is: why Austin has used the terms constative and performative? Why not he used some other terms? Well, when Austin has used the term constative, he also pondered over some other terms, like *informative* and *descriptive*. However, these terms are not as accurate as Austin desired. He needed a term whose meaning would be radically different from the performative utterances. Informative is an extensive term and is used for all kinds of information, knowledge and so forth. *'The Chambers Dictionary'* defines it as "having the power to form."[7] The term constative is used for an assertion, especially to contrast with performative utterance. According to *'The Chambers Dictionary'*, *constative* means, "(of a statement) that can be true or false; that implies assertion rather than performance—*in* such a statement (opposed to *performative*)."[8] While, *'The Oxford Advanced Learner's Dictionary'*, defines constative as "stating that something is real or true."[9] Hence, the term constative is well-defined and is used in a definite sense which the term *informative* lacks.

Austin also considered the term *descriptive* and differentiated it from the constative. As he writes, "It has come to be seen that many especially perplexing words embedded in apparently descriptive statements do not serve to indicate some specially odd additional feature in the reality reported, but to indicate (not to report) the circumstances in which the statement is made or reservations to which it is subject or the way in which it is to be taken and the like. To overlook these possibilities in the way once common is called the 'descriptive' fallacy; but perhaps this is not a good name, as 'descriptive' itself is special. Not all true or false statements are descriptions, and for this reason I prefer to use the word 'Constative'."[10] On this account, Austin uses the term *constative inter alia* informative and descriptive.

Likewise, Austin preferred to use the term performatives, in place of some other alternatives like *operative*. The word operative is used in a very wide sense. For instance, it has always been used by lawyers in their legal proceedings. The word operative demands some legal evidence or document, so that in the absence of evidence we can't use this word. Indeed, the term operative is more legal than the performative. As Austin wrote, "This is rather an ugly word, and a new word, but there seems to be no word already in existence to do the job. The nearest approach that I can think of is the word *operative*, as used by lawyers. Lawyers when talking about legal instruments will distinguish between the preamble, which recites the circumstances in which a transaction is effected, and on the other hand the operative part—the part of it which actually performs the legal act which is the purpose of the instrument to perform. So the word operative is very near to what we want....... However, the word operative has other uses, and it seems preferable to have a word specially designed for the use we want."[11]

Austin further gave numerous down to earth examples for the identification of performatives like:[12]

(a) 'I do (sc. take this woman to be my lawful wedded wife)'—as uttered in the course of the marriage ceremony.
(b) 'I name this ship the Queen Elizabeth'—as uttered when smashing the bottle against the stem.
(c) 'I give and bequeath my watch to my brother'—as occurring in a wall.
(d) 'I bet you six pence it will rain tomorrow.'

All these examples indeed perform some act rather than state or describe some fact. Hence, these are not true or false but happy or unhappy. For instance, when I say that I name this ship the Queen Elizabeth, I do not describe the christening ceremony. Of course, I am naming this ship. Likewise, when I say before the registrar that 'I do this woman my lawful wedded spouse', then I am not reporting or describing the report of a marriage. Indeed, I am indulging in it and thereby I accept an unmarried woman as my legal wife. Moreover, when I say that 'I give and bequeath my watch to my brother', by saying this I am not informing someone about my watch or my brother, but actually, I give my watch to my brother. In addition, when I say that I bet you six pence it will rain tomorrow, then in reality I perform the act of betting *inter alia* merely saying or reporting about the process of bet. Precisely, all these examples are powerful examples of performative utterance, which have always been used to perform some acts rather than merely saying something.

The question is that why Austin has chosen these particular type of examples in the *same grammatical form—first person, singular number, present tense and indicative sentences?* Of Course, Austin's aim was to show that there are numerous utterances which superficially sound like statements in terms of describing or informing some fact but these are not statement in that sense. These are always used to perform some acts *vis-à-vis* to do something. By virtue of this, Austin considered the examples of similar grammatical forms.

Now, let me suppose that if a person at random utters that 'I do'. Can I say that this utterance is performative? According to Austin, for happy performatives, it is indispensable that our utterance must be in appropriate language and it should be uttered by an appropriate person in appropriate circumstances and all the participants who are involved in this procedure perform their act with honesty and sincerity (both mentally and physically). For instance, when I say, 'I do this woman as my lawful wedded spouse'. For the successful performance of this act, it is inevitable that I should not already be married with a wife; living, sane, undivorced woman. If all these conditions (objective as well as subjective) are fulfilled, this utterance will successfully perform the act of marriage. Infringement of any of these conditions will make our utterances infelicitous and eventually this will be called unhappy. Austin conceived that if an utterance will not perform act, the utterance will not be false but unhappy to the extent that truth or falsity is the characteristic of the constative utterance but not the characteristic of performative utterance. As he said, ".......the utterance is then, we may say, not indeed false but in general unhappy. And for this reason we call the doctrine of the things that can be and go wrong on the occasion of such utterances, the doctrine of the infelicities."[13]

Austin, therefore, sets out the following touchstones which are *sine qua non* for smooth or happy functioning of performatives:

(A1) "There must exist an accepted conventional procedure having a certain conventional effect, that procedure to include the uttering of certain words by certain persons in certain circumstances."[14] For example, 'I divorce you', said thrice to his wife by Hindus and Christians, would not be performative. There are no such procedures in the Hindu and Christian mythology to divorce his wife by merely verbal saying. However, if Mohammedans use these words for their spouses, this utterance must perform the act of divorce. In the Islam religion, there is a legal procedure that if you like to divorce your wife, merely say thrice 'I divorce you.' Likewise, on a desert island if someone orders me to 'Go and pick up wood' and I say "I don't take order from you' or you are not entitled to give me order inasmuch as you are not an authorised person or captain. Plainly, in a desert island, only the captain of a ship can order. In such a situation, this utterance will not be performative.

(A2) "The particular persons and circumstances in a given case must be appropriate for the invocation of the particular procedure invoked."[15] For example, 'I appoint you', said when I have already been appointed or when you are not such a appointing authority. Similarly, when a person says with a horse 'I do you my lawful wedded spouse', then the act of marriage will not performed. Precisely, the particular person (horse) is not appropriate person for marriage to the extent that there are prohibited degrees of relationship between a man and a horse.

(B1) "The procedure must be executed by all participants correctly."[16] For instance, I say, 'I bet you the race won't be run today'. If more than one race is arranged, the procedure is not executed correctly. Another example may be, if a man says to a young woman walking in the street, 'I do you my lawful wedded spouse'. This utterance will not perform the act of marriage. Of course, there is certain procedure for marriage in diverse religions and this procedure must be followed by the person indulging in this process.

(B2) "The procedure must be executed by all participants completely."[17] For example, I said that 'I bet you six pence'. This utterance will be in vain unless you don't say 'I take you on.' Here, the process is not completely fulfilled inasmuch as the person does not give any response in the favour of bet.

Furthermore, Austin claimed that in all likelihood, the circumstances are in order, the person who are involved in this procedure are also appropriate and the act executed correctly as well as completely by the person. Instead, the feeling, thought and intention of the person may not be real. The act, therefore, will not be happily performed. On this account, Austin assumed that the speaker should internally indulge in the whole processes for the successful performance. Hence, he bestows some other criteria (in addition to the above) for the successful performance:

(T1) "Where, as often, the procedure is designed for use by persons having certain thoughts or feelings, or for the inauguration of certain consequential conduct on the part of any participant, then a person participating in and so invoking the procedure must in fact have those thoughts or feelings, and the participants must intend so to conduct themselves."[18] In this characterisation, Austin pleads in favour of subjectivity like intention, thought and feeling of the speaker. For instance, when I say 'I congratulate you' instead I do not feel pleased at all, or even I am annoyed. Likewise, 'I promise' when I do not intend to promise.

(T2) "And the participant must actually so conduct themselves subsequently."[19]

While commenting upon the above these six touchstones, Austin said that firstly, these rules are not complete. They can be reduced and increased. Secondly, these rules are not only useful for philosophy but also for sciences, mathematics and so forth. Thirdly, these touchstones can be applied for all ceremonial activities. Finally, the classification of these instances hinge upon our intelligence as to how do we classify it? As he wrote, "I claimed (1) that it applied to all ceremonial acts, not merely verbal ones, and that these are more common than is appreciated; I admitted (2) that our list was not complete, and that there are indeed other whole dimensions of what might be reasonably called unhappiness affecting ceremonial performances in general and utterances in general, dimensions which are certainly the concern of philosophers; and (3) that, of course, different infelicities can be combined or can overlap and that it can be more or less an optional matter how we classify some given particular example."[20]

If we sin against anyone (or more) of these six rules, our utterances must be unhappy or infelicitous. In the above rules, Austin emphasised on both *verbal* as well as *non-verbal* procedure for the happy or smooth performatives. Over and above, he distinguished between the four rules (A1-B2) and the last two rules (T1-T2). Rules (A1-B2) are underpinned over the *objectivity*, while the later two rules (T1-T2) are based upon *subjectivity*. The former are such criteria which are merely verbal. If any fault occurs in these conditions, our utterances will be *Misfire*, while the latter are such criteria which are non-verbal and concerned with the intention, thought, and feeling of the speaker; if any fault occurs in these rules, our utterance will be infelicitous which Austin called *Abuse*. When the utterance is Misfire, the procedure which we follow will be *disallowed* or *botched* and our act will be *empty* or without effect. In the cases of T infelicitous act will be called as *professed* or *hollow* rather than *purported* or *empty*. Further, Austin distinguished between the cases A and the cases B. About the A cases, Austin asserted that either there is no such procedure or the procedure exists alright but cannot be applied as purported. Such types of infelicities are called *Misinvocation,* while the procedure exists but can't be applied is purported may be called *Misapplication*. While in the case of B, the conventional procedure must exist, it can also be applied very well, but we muff the execution of the ritual with more or less dire consequences. So, the B cases as opposed to A cases will be called Misexecution as opposed to Misinvocation: the purported act is vitiated by a Flaw or Hitch in the conduct of the ceremony. The class (B1) is that of *Flaws*, the class (B2) that of *Hitches*. He further, distinguished between T1 and T2 cases. In the case of T1 if feelings and intentions are not real then the utterances will be *insincerities* but in the T2 cases, Austin said if we sin against it, our utterances will be *infractions* or *breaches*. The following scheme's of Austin may elucidate the above infelicities:

**INFELICITIES**

AB<br>Misfires<br>Act purported<br>but void

T<br>Abuses<br>Act professed<br>but hollow

A<br>Misinvocations<br>Act disallowed

A1<br>?

A2<br>Misapplication

B<br>Misexecutions<br>Act vitiated

B1<br>Flaws

B2<br>Hitches

T1<br>Insincerities

T2<br>?

J.O. Urmson[21] remarks that Austin from time to time used other names for the different infelicities. For instance, A1, Non-plays; A2—Misplays; B—Miscarriages; B1—Misexecutions; B2—Non-executions; T—Disrespects; T1—Dissimulations; T2—Non-fulfilments, Disloyalties, Infractions, Indisciplines, Breaches.

Now, an important question arises as to how may we identify the performative utterances? Austin suggests two noteworthy touchstones:

- Grammatical Criterion;
- Vocabulary Criterion.

*Grammatical Criterion*: "........ *use of verb in the first person singular present indicative active*."[22] For example, I name, I bet, I do, I give and so forth. If a person asserts, I do, or I bet, then he does not describe or report of his act, indeed he performs these acts. Austin conceived that there are some important asymmetry between this person and tense with other person and tense. For instance, 'I promise' and 'I promised' or 'he promises'. Although, all the three assertions are superficially similar, notwithstanding, these are different in their mould or character. When a person utters 'I promised' or 'he promises', he is simply describing or reporting of his promise. However, when a person states 'I promise', he is not reporting or describing of his promise but indeed he does promise. It reveals that when a person says 'I promise', it insinuates his/her commitment about his utterance. However, when a person says 'I promised' or 'he promises', the commitment of the speaker about this utterance is somehow feasible or weak. While giving an interesting example Austin wrote, "......thus a clear difference between our first person singular present indicative active, and other persons and tenses. This is brought out by the typical incident of little Willie whose uncle says he'll give him half-a-crown if he promises never to smoke until he's 55. Little Willie's anxious parent will say 'of course he promises, don't you, Willie?' giving him a nudge and little Willie just doesn't vouchsafe. The point here is that he must do the promising himself by saying 'I promise,' and his parent is going too fast in saying 'he promises'."[23]

*Vocabulary Criterion*—use of the word *hereby*. "Hereby is a useful criterion that the utterance is performative."[24] Again, Austin took *'hereby'* or some equivalent—as in French, the phrase *'par ces mots-ci'*,[25] as a useful criterion for happy performative. For example, notice is hereby given that the trespasser will be prosecuted. Albeit, the form of this utterance is not in the first person, singular, present, indicative, active, nonetheless this utterance is not less performative. By virtue of this, Austin emphasized on the use of the word, *hereby*.

While explaining this, J.R. Searle wrote, "I think we use *hereby* because 'I promise' and 'I hereby promise' are amongst function-indicating devices for *commitment* provided by English language. For that reason we often use these expressions in the performance of speech acts which are not strictly speaking promises but in which we wish to emphasize our commitment."[26] Searle, therefore, thinks that 'hereby' is a specific word used in the English speaking world for explicit performative utterances.

Later, Austin felt some problems in the above touchstones. He, therefore, brushed aside these touchstones and argued that we may also get some utterances in the second and third person and even in the passive voice. "..........where the verb is in the passive voice and in the second or in the third person, not in the first."[27] For instance, 'You are hereby authorised to do so and so' or 'Passengers are warned to cross the track by the bridge only'. The above examples are undoubtedly 'performatives', while their form is not in the first person singular present indicative active. Austin, moreover, assumed that the verb may be even *impersonal*.[28] For instance, 'Notice is hereby given that the trespassers will be prosecuted'. This utterance is of course performative.

Austin agreed that there is no exact criterion for performatives. Any utterance which is in the form of 'first person, singular, present, indicative active' can be corrigible or can be reducible or expandable. "Still, it is doubtful whether this is a grammatical criterion exactly (what is?), and anyway it is not very exact."[29] Warnock argued that on the one hand, an utterance may be in the 'first person, singular, present, indicative active yet this utterance will not be performative at all. On the other hand, there are some utterances which are not under this criterion, still these are performative. ".......is there 'some grammatical (or lexicographical) criterion for distinguishing the performative utterances?' It takes him little time, as indeed it should, to find that the answer is negative. The examples he has so far cited of performative utterance have, as it happens, been of a particular form—first person, singular, present indicative active, as in 'I name this ship.....' 'I bet you sixpence.....,' 'I promise .......'. That, however, clearly affords no sort of general criterion. For an utterance, he remarks, may be performative but not in that form: instead of 'I give you permission to go.' I may say simply 'You may go'; and an utterance may be in that form but not performative: 'I vote for the Liberal' may be, not voting for the Liberal, but simply stating what I habitually do when I vote. (This, of course, was the very first point that Austin made—a performative utterance may be formally exactly like a constative). Even more obviously, there is no help to be found in individual words—" 'I promise', 'I bet' may be performative, but certainly not just because of the occurrence of 'promise' and 'bet'; for 'He promises'; 'They bet' are very clearly not performative in the way that the first-person utterances are."[30]

Over and above, Austin concedes therefore that performative utterance may be without the use of the verb *hereby*. For instance, Passengers are warned to cross the track by bridge only; You are ordered to follow these rules; You are authorized to do so and so, and the like. Precisely, these examples are performatives. However, they do not comprise the term *hereby*.

In addition, there are some other problems with this term. Firstly, *hereby*, is not a specific word which is merely used by English speaking person as Searle believed. More or less, it has been used in all conventions in the same sense especially for *legal proceedings*. According to *New Oxford Advanced Learner's Dictionary* (2005), the meaning of the term *hereby* is "(*in legal documents*, etc.) as a result of this statement, and in a way that makes something *legal*."[31] Austin, himself writes, "The 'hereby' formula is a useful alternative; but it is rather *too formal* for ordinary purposes."[32]

Secondly, as the term 'hereby' has always been used for the functioning of the legal proceedings, it naturally demands some written documents. Austin himself wrote, "Very typical of this kind of performative—especially liable to occur in *written documents* of course—is that the little word 'hereby' either actually occurs or might naturally be inserted."[33]

Thirdly, there are many cases, when the speaker utters something without using the word *hereby*; however its performativity is indubitable. If the speaker of the parliament, for instance, utters 'this house (parliament) is adjourned', then only this utterance is adequate for the adjournment of the house (parliament) and there is no need to use the word *hereby*. Apart from this, we may consider a couple of examples. Suppose a jury simply says that the court is adjourned without using the word *hereby*. Likewise, a groom says in the church before a priest that I accept this woman as my lawful wedded spouse. Can we say that these utterances are less than performative? Precisely, these utterances are performatives and also ample *per se* to perform these acts. It is, therefore, my conviction that in a certain convention, without using the word *hereby*, the act must perform.

Fourthly, it may be possible that the speaker uses the term *hereby* yet he may be insincere about his commitment. In the legal proceedings, the question of the sincerity or insincerity does not arise inasmuch as at that floor performatives work in accordance with certain rules. Even if the speaker may be insincere about his commitment, the act must perform in accordance with certain objective rules. The problem of sincerity or insincerity arises only in the case of informal situations, *i.e.*, when there are no certain rules. It is, therefore, my conviction that the term *hereby* is useful only in the case of legal proceedings. In addition to legal proceedings, it is unable to reveal the sincerity of the speaker. It is not sufficient to say that this is the *breach of commitment*. Whenever, we speak about the functions of language, we will have to consider its all facets.

Fifthly, in all likelihood, the speaker uses the term *hereby*; yet he may hide his *real intention* and report a *hidden intention*. For example, it is a well known fact that Pakistan is involved in terrorist activities and infiltrations in India, especially in Jammu and Kashmir. The Indian government has been persistently providing its evidence. The President of Pakistan, however, brushes aside this fact and affirms that Pakistan is not involved in such activities. Even, the American President knows this fact; however, he has always expressed his ignorance of this fact and attempts to show his keen interest in resolving the problem of terrorism. The president of U.S.A. repeatedly utters, *I hereby assure that the terrorist activities should end across the world*. Instead, he is not interested in resolving the problem of terrorism in India. By virtue of the above complexity, we may say that hereby can't be a adequate criterion for performatives.

Sixthly, the term *hereby* has not been always used to perform some acts. Sometimes, it may be used to describe or inform something, like, 'I hereby inform you that Prof. X is appointed as a chairman of the University Grants Commission.' Indeed, this utterance is descriptive or informative *vis-à-vis* performative.

Searle was aware of this fact and therefore, he openly holds, "I find the statement of the conditions very difficult to do, and I am not entirely satisfied with the list I am about to present. One reason for the difficulty is that the notion of promise, like most notions in ordinary language, does not have absolutely strict rules. There are all sorts of odd, deviants, and borderline promises; and counter examples, more or less bizarre, can be produced against my analysis. I am inclined to think we shall not be able to get a set of knock-down *necessary* and *sufficient* conditions that will exactly mirror the ordinary use of the word 'hereby'."[34]

In this regard, Austin rightly claimed that there is no *exact* criterion for performatives. "This reduces us to an impasse over any *single simple* criterion of grammar or vocabulary. But may be it is not impossible to produce a complex criterion, or at least a set of criteria, simple or complex, involving both grammar and vocabulary. For example, one of the criteria might be that everything with the verb in the imperative mood is performative."[35] Besides, "Any utterance which is performative could be reduced, or expanded, or analyzed into one of these two standard forms, beginning 'I......' so and so or beginning 'You (or he) hereby.......' so and so."[36] Eventually, Austin says, "The first suggestion was a criterion or a criteria of grammar or of vocabulary or of both. We pointed out that there was certainly no one absolute criterion of this kind; and that very probably it is not possible to lay down even a list of all possible criteria; moreover, they certainly would not distinguish performatives and constatives, as very commonly the *same* sentence is used on different occasions of utterance in *both* ways, performative and constative."[37] Austin is, therefore, unable to sustain the distinction between the constative and the performative utterance for long spell.

He moreover suggested another criterion which plainly distinguishes the performatives into two sorts: Primary or Implicit performative utterances and Explicit performative utterances. Here, it is important to mention that Dieter Wunderlich[38] distinguishes performative utterance into two sorts: *Primary Performative Utterances* (*e.g., shut up*) and *Secondary Performative Utterances* (*e.g., I hereby demand......*). The following examples should be helpful:

(i) "Primary or Implicit performative: 'I shall be there'.
(ii) Explicit performative: 'I promise that I shall be there', and we said that the latter formula made explicit what action it is that is being performed in issuing the utterance: *i.e.* 'I shall be there'."[39]

Austin moreover suggested two caveats, for explicit performative utterances. The first, explicit performative utterances are those utterances which do not describe or state something, rather they perform something. It incorporates many other things, like: *the tone of voice, cadence, gesture, the nature of circumstances and the context* in which an utterance takes place. Austin also conceived that explicit performative utterances are liked *non-linguistic action* rather than linguistic. For example, bending before you, I remove my cap, sweeping my other hand to my heart and uttering some noise or words perhaps *Salam,* then the uttering *Salam* is not more than describing my performance, but undoubtedly, I am performing my act of obeisance. In the same way, when I say, 'I promise' or 'I Warn you that........,' these utterances are not describing about promising or warning inasmuch as 'I promise' makes it unambiguously a promise.

Secondly, it is necessary that the utterances should be in the form of *that* clause. It may be used in the form of 'indirect speech', which plainly insinuates something else rather than myself. "........although we have in this type of utterance a 'that'-clause following a verb, for example 'promise', or 'fid' or 'pronounce' (or perhaps such verbs as 'estimate'), we must not allude to this as 'indirect speech.' 'That'-clauses in indirect speech *ordatio obliqua* are, of course, cases where I report what someone else or myself else when or elsewhere did say: .........Incidentally, of course, it is not in the least necessary that an explicit performative verb should be followed by 'that': in important classes of cases it is followed by 'to ......' or nothing, for example, 'I apologize (for ......),' 'I salute you'."[40]

Over and above, Austin distinguished between the implicit performative utterances and the explicit performative utterances, on basically two grounds. Firstly, historically, the explicit performative utterances must be later development rather than implicit performative. For example, 'I will...', is earlier than 'I promise...' Secondly, the former marks clearly the *force* of the utterances, whereas the later emphasises on the *meaning* of the utterances. So, implicit performatives are not as clear as explicit performatives. Implicit performative contains ambiguity, vagueness, equivocation and so on. For example, if someone asserts 'Bull', then the question may arise as to what he would like to say by the utterance 'Bull'? It may be a warning, or an information or a prediction also. Thus, there is no certainty of meaning in this word 'Bull'. While clarity and certainty is indispensable for the explicit performative. Austin himself conceded that clarification is as much a creative acts as a discovery or description.

The question is; how shall we identify the explicit performatives? Austin pointed out four touchstones for the identifications of explicit performative utterances. These are followings:

(A) "Whether it makes sense to say 'Does he really'?
(B) Whether one could really be doing it without actually saying anything?
(C) Can we qualify the putative performative with the idea of 'being willing to' and 'deliberately'?
(D) Whether what one says could be literally false, or only insincere?"[41]

Austin admitted that the implication is that if the utterances in question are genuinely performative then the answer of the question (A), (B) and (D) will be negative, while the answer of (C) will be affirmative.

However, Austin was doubtful about the above criterion. As Keith Graham commented, "Austin clearly has misgivings about these tests, however, and rightly so. Even if someone uses an uncontroversial performative formula, such as, 'I promise....', it will still make sense to ask whether he did really, because it is also necessary for the felicity conditions to be met. Again, Austin himself points out that we often can perform the same kind of action as done in uttering a performative, but by some other means. I can bet, for example, by putting a coin into a slot machine. These uncertainties reflect Austin's lack of clarity in his own conception of a performative. This applies equally to question (D). Performatives, I shall argue, can be true or false, this will not help to distinguish them either."[42]

Thus, Austin felt that all the above distinctions of the constative and the performative utterance or the implicit performative and the explicit performative, are untenable. Every utterance is both the constative and the performative. So, we can't draw a borderline between the constative and the performative, as we can't distinguish the existence of twilight between day and night. For example, 'I hold that ......', when said by a judge, will be performative, while in the case of layman, we can't say so. An another example, 'I class x's as y's', which may be performative on the one occasion and it can be constative also on the other occasions. The worst example is that 'I state that p' which is straightforwardly both, the constative and the performative.

Finally, Austin comprehended three other cases, which are as follows:

(i) Someone says 'All John's children are bald, but John has no children.' In other words, 'All John's children are bald', when, as a matter of fact, John has no children.
(ii) Someone says, 'The cat is on the mat', but I don't believe it is, *i.e.*, 'The cat is on the mat', when as a matter of fact, he does not believe it is.

(iii) Someone says 'All the guests are French' and some of them are not or perhaps he says 'All the guests are French', and then he says 'Some of the guests are not French.'

"In each of these cases one experiences a feeling of outrage, and it's possible each time for us to try to express it in terms of the same word—implication, or perhaps that word that we always find so handy, contradiction. But there are more ways of killing the cat than drawing it in butter, and equally, to do violence to language one does not always need a contradiction."[43]

Let us consider three terms *presuppose, imply* and *entail* for above three cases, respectively. For the first case, 'John's children are bald' or 'John's children are not bald' *presupposes* that John has children, *viz.*, we cannot say anything about these children, without acceptance of their existence. Firstly, they exist and then they are bald or not bald. In the same way, the cat is on the mat, *implies* that I believe it, *viz.*, we may not say that the cat is on the mat but I don't believe it. Likewise, in the third case, all the guests are French *entails* that some of guests are also French.

While, Austin considered these statements in a different way. If someone says 'All John's children are bald but John has no children.' It may be an outrageous thing to say but it is not self-contradictory. Only we may say that this statement (John's children are bald) is meaningless or void due to lack of reference or ambiguity of reference. This case is similar to that situation in which a person contracts with other person to sell a piece of land but as a matter of fact, he has no land. In such a situation, this negotiation must be *infringement* or *void* due to lack of reference. Likewise, the statement that all John's children are bald but John has no children, is void due to lack of proper reference.

In the Second case, 'The cat is on the mat, but I don't believe it.' According to Austin, this statement is also not self-contradictory like the first. There is lack of *insincerity* involved in it. In the same way, when someone asserts that 'I promise that I shall be there' but as a ground reality, he has no intention to promise. If one is not sincere about his/her commitment, this statement will not be false but it indicates the lack of sincerity which makes a peculiar kind of nonsense.

Eventually, in the third case, 'All the guests are French, but some of the guests are not French.' This statement is also not self-contradictory but there is a *breach of commitment*. This statement is similar to that statement, when some one says, 'I welcome you', instead he has the least intention to welcome or even that he behaves like an enemy or an intruder. Indeed, these sorts of utterances indicate the insincerity of the person, so that these utterances are not false but a certain kind of nonsense. At the surface, these statements sound like constative which may be either true or false. But as a ground reality, these statements are not true or false but these are in the form of felicitous or infelicitous.

In this regard, Austin endeavoured to prove that the distinction between the constative and the performative utterances is not appropriate. On the one, the constative utterances may be felicitous or infelicitous, like performative utterances. Performative utterances, on the other, also may be true or false, like constative utterances. Austin, therefore, brushed aside this distinction and enunciated a new doctrine of utterances, known as speech act theory. In the words of Austin, "So far I have called attention to two things: that there is no purely verbal criterion by which to distinguish the performative from the constative utterance, and that the constative is liable to the same unhappiness as the performative. Now we must ask ourselves whether issuing a constative utterance is not, after all, the performance of an act, the act, namely, of stating. Is stating an act in the same sense as marrying, apologizing, betting, etc.? I can't plumb this mystery any further at present. But it is already pretty evident that the formula 'I state that .......' is closely similar to the formula 'I Warm you that .......'—a formula which, as we put it, serves to make explicit what speech act, it is that we are performing; and also, that one can't issue any utterance whatever without performing some speech-act of this kind. What we need, perhaps, is a more general theory of these speech-acts, and in this theory our constative-performative antithesis will scarcely survive."[44]

Later, while giving varied sorts of examples, Keith Graham endeavoured to justify this distinction. He believed that Austin's contention that each utterance is constative and performative, is untenable. "I shall now argue that Austin's despair was premature. I shall attempt to show that it is possible to characterize performatives in such a way that they can be regarded as a distinct type of utterance."[45]

Earlier I have seen that the distinction between the constative and the performative utterance is doing and saying. In addition, the form of constative utterance is true or false, while, the form of performative utterance is felicitous or infelicitous. If there is a fact in accordance with an utterance, the utterance will be true. Graham gives some examples whose truth don't hinge upon its corresponding fact. These utterances guarantee their truth in *per se*. While, there are some other utterances which don't guarantee their truth in itself to the extent that their facts are independent of these utterances. Graham, for instance, considered the three following statements:

(1) I am alive.
(2) I am saying something.
(3) I am speaking in English.

On the one hand, these utterances are superficially similar to each other due to their self-verifying character, on the other hand, these are different also. In the first case, whatever I will ask, would be true, even if I don't ask anything at all. While for the second and the third cases, it is *sine qua non* that we say something. In that respect, the first case is different *inter alia* the rest two cases. It doesn't reveal that the second and the third cases are similar to each other. These are different also due to their verifiable character. For instance, for the second case, merely saying is ample *per se*. Whatever I am saying, is not important. While the truth of the third case is in very restricted sense. This utterance will be true if and only if we speak in English. Apart from, Graham assumed that the truth of the second and the third cases are different from the first to the extent that their truth doesn't depend upon itself like the first.

Graham, furthermore, compared these statements with another performative utterances, *viz.*, 'I promise........' this utterance will be true if there will be a fact in accordance with it. In such situation, I promise is on a par with the second and the third rather than the first to the extent that if we prise them off from the situations, it will be no longer true. Instead, there are difference between 'I promise' and the two cases. The second and the third cases are self-verifying, while, 'I promise' is verifiable in respect of other situations. Here it is important to mention that E.J. Lemmon,[46] in his formulation, *On Sentences Verifiable by their Use*, holds that *I promise* (such and such), is also verifiable by its use and therefore, it is like a statement. Lemmon, therefore, advocated that I promise (such and such), as a self-verifiable statement, likewise, I am speaking now.

Precisely, the situation regarding allowable substitute is varied for the diverse utterances. As Graham wrote, "However, in two other respects performatives differ from all three utterances. First, where the allowable substitution is of another utterance, there is a much stricter limitation than for (1)—(3). To make it true that I promise there is little else that I can *say* besides uttering the words which identify that performative, or synonymous form of words (or, say, uttering the word 'yes' in reply to the question 'Do you promise?'). That is to say, the content of a performative utterance is for more germane than the case with (1)—(3). Secondly, we saw that the utterance of (1)—(3) was, in the fairly straightforward way, sufficient for their truth. Not so with performatives. There is the additional, crucial requirement that the performative be uttered in the appropriate circumstances, or that the felicity—conditions, associated with it be fulfilled. Saying 'I promise.......' Does not make it true that I promise if no one around to hear; saying 'I bet.........' Does not make it true that I bet if no one takes me up."[47]

Graham, moreover, considered on three other utterances and compared with the above three utterances (1)—(3). The specific characteristics of these utterances is that the facts of these utterances are entirely separate from these utterances. It may seem that their truth hinges upon certain fact, while as a matter of fact, their truth does not depend upon some other facts. Graham gives three other instances and shows this complexity. "Imagine, a teacher carrying a delicate balance across a school laboratory. Just as he passes, a pupil shouts out at the top of his voice:

(4) 'you have dropped it!'

The utterance is delivered so suddenly and at such a volume that its own truth is thereby assured. Next another malicious pedagogic relationship. A student is on the point of entering an examination room. His tutor, who happens to be invigilating, says to him,

(5) 'you will fail this examination'.

Ill-prepared and unconfident though the student was, he would have just scraped through the examination had this remark not been made. Finally, in a newspaper column highly regarded for its accuracy as a barometer of the market, it is started with that,

(6) 'The price of the gold will fall tomorrow.'

As a consequence, the price of the gold does indeed fall the following days."[48]

If we compare both the cases (1—3) and (4—6), then we clearly find some differences. The former three (1—3) are self-verifying, while the latter three (4—6) are verifiable in respect of some other contexts to the extent that the fact of these utterances is separate from it. For instance, the fourth might be true that the teacher dropped the balance by pushing him. Similarly, the sixth might be true due to the assassination of the Prime Minister. While, in the fifth 'you will fail in the examination', might be true that the student will pass the examination. Thus, the truth of these utterances is entirely separate from their facts inasmuch as these utterances require something else besides the fulfilment of felicitous conditions. "The respective statements play a role in bringing about some separate state of affairs which is constitutive of their truth, whether in a relatively brute fashion as in (4), or through the mediation of the hearer's understanding and belief as in (5) and (6)."[49]

By virtue of above discussion, Graham endeavoured to distinguish between the constative and the performative utterances. The constative utterances are neither equivalent to

(1—3), as self-verifying nor similar to (4—6), with separate fact from these utterances. Graham conceived as to the performatives bring out their truth from the social context. In the varied social contexts, the performatives perform varied acts. On this account Graham argued that the performatives work not only in accordance with their meaning but also their *contexts*. In the both cases, the latter are more important than the earlier. "The performative utterance does not bring about a substantially separate state of affairs which is responsible from its truth, as in (4)—(6), but neither is it logically sufficient for its own truth, as in (1)—(3). It *conventionally* brings about its own truth in the following sense: the content expressed by the utterance becomes true when the statements—act is performed *because people regard* it as being so as a consequence of the act of the utterance. To put it this way is to emphasise that the existence of performatives rests not only on utterance but also upon social attitudes....... If people did not adopt the attitude they do towards a person who says 'I promise.....' (and they are not force to), then 'I promise.......' Could not be self-verifying in the way in which it is. We may put this in the form of a definition by saying that a statement—act S is performative if and only if it brings about the truth of the content it express as a consequence of people's so regarding it."[50]

When we ponder over Graham's contention, we may say that Graham is not concerned with the distinction between the constative and the performative utterance. Actually, his argument is concerned with *how performatives works*. On this account, he provides varied sorts of example and endeavoured to show that in different situations its truth underpins upon varied facts.

The above discourse highlights the fact that there is not a certain or definite criterion which gracefully may distinguish between the constative and the performative utterance. An utterance has been used in both the senses, *i.e.*, an utterance not only describes or states something but also performs something. The distinction between the constative and the performative is, therefore, finally abolished. By virtue of this,

Austin brushed aside this distinction and argued in the favour of speech act theory.

## REFERENCES


1. Austin, J.L. (1980): *How to Do Things with Words.* J.O. Urmson and M. Sbisa (Ed.), p. 3
2. *Ibid.* p. 5
3. Warnock, G.J. (1989): *J.L. Austin*, p. 108.
4. Cerf, Walter. (1969): *Critical Review of How to Do Things with Words.* In K.T. Funn; Symposium on J.L. Austin (Ed.), p. 351.
5. Chisholm, R.M. (1969): *Austin's Philosophical Papers.* In K.T. Fann (Ed) Symposium on J.L. Austin p. 111.
6. Graham, Keith (1977): *J.L. Austin: A Critique of Ordinary Language Philosophy.* pp. 57-58.
7. See, '*The Chambers Dictionary*' (2004): Edited by Sandra Anderson, Linda Carey and others, Published by Allied Chambers (India) Limited, New Delhi, p. 824.
8. *Ibid.* p. 350.
9. See, '*The New Oxford Advanced Learner's Dictionary*' (2005): Edited by Sally Wehmeier, Published by Oxford University Press, printed in India, p. 326.
10. Austin, J.L. (1982): *How to Do Things with Words*, J.O. Urmson and M. Sbisa (Ed), p. 3.
11. Austin, J.L. (1979): *Philosophical Papers.* In J.O. Urmson and G.J. Warnock (Ed.). pp. 235-36.
12. Austin, J.L. (1980): *How to Do Things with Words.* J.O. Urmson and M. Sbisa (Ed.), p. 5.
13. *Ibid.* p. 14.
14. *Ibid.* p. 14.
15. *Ibid.* p. 15.
16. *Ibid.* p. 15.
17. *Ibid.* p. 15.
18. *Ibid.* p. 15.
19. *Ibid.* p. 15.
20. *Ibid.* pp. 25-26.
21. *Ibid.* p. 18.
22. *Ibid.* p. 56.
23. Austin, J.L (1979): '*Performative Utterance*', J.O. Urmson and G.J. Warnock (Ed), 'Philosophical Papers', p. 242.
24. Austin, J.L. (1980): *How to Do Things with Words.* J.O. Urmson and M. Sbisa (Ed.), p. 57.

25. Austin, J.L. (1963): *'Performative-Constative'*, Searle, J. R. (1979): *'The Philosophy of Language'*(Ed), p. 15.
26. Searle, J.R. (1979): *'The Philosophy of Language'*(Ed), p. 49.
27. Austin, J.L (1979): *'Performative Utterance'*, J.O. Urmson and G.J. Warnock (Ed), 'Philosophical Papers' p. 242.
28. Austin, J.L. (1982): *How to Do Things with Words*, J.O. Urmson and M. Sbisa (Ed), p. 57.
29. *Ibid.* pp. 63-64.
30. Warnock, G.J. (1989): *J.L. Austin*, pp. 115-16.
31. See, *'The New Oxford Advanced Learner's Dictionary'* (2005) edited by Sally Wehmeier, Published by Oxford University Press, printed in India, p. 728.
32. Austin, J.L (1979): *'Performative Utterance'*, J.O. Urmson and G.J. Warnock (Ed), 'Philosophical Papers' p. 243.
33. *Ibid.* pp. 242-43.
34. Searle, J.R. (1979): *'The Philosophy of Language'*(Ed), p. 47.
35. Austin, J.L. (1982): *How to Do Things with Words*, J.O. Urmson and M. Sbisa (Ed), p. 59.
36. Austin, J.L (1979): *'Performative Utterance'*, J.O. Urmson and G.J. Warnock (Ed), 'Philosophical Papers' p. 243.
37. Austin, J.L. (1982): *How to Do Things with Words*, J.O. Urmson and M. Sbisa (Ed), p. 67.
38. See, Wunderlich, Dieter (1974): *'Foundations of Linguistics'*, Translated in English from the German *Grundlelagen der Linguistik* by Roger Loss in 1979, p. 268.
39. Austin, J.L. (1980): *How to Do Things with Words*. J.O. Urmson and M. Sbisa (Ed.), p. 69.
40. *Ibid.* pp. 70-71.
41. *Ibid.* pp. 79-80.
42. Graham, Keith (1977): *J.L. Austin: A Critique of Ordinary Language Philosophy*. pp. 64-65.
43. Warnock, G.J. (1979): *Performative—Constative*. In J. R. Searle: Philosophy of Language (Ed.), p. 17.
44. *Ibid.* p. 20.
45. Graham, Keith (1977): *J.L. Austin: A critique of Ordinary Language Philosophy*, p. 67.
46. Lemmon, E.J. (1962): *On Sentences Verifiable by their Use Analysis*, Vol. 22, No. 4. pp. 86-89.
47. Graham, Keith (1977): *J.L. Austin: A critique of Ordinary Language Philosophy*, p. 70.
48. *Ibid.* pp. 70-71.
49. *Ibid.* p. 71.
50. *Ibid.* pp. 75-76.

# 4

# Why to Distinguish Performative and Constative Utterances?

Austin is one of those philosophers who firstly propounded his doctrine about utterances and later, he rejected it. In his earlier formulation, he distinguished between two sorts of utterances: the constative and the performative. He, however, felt some mistakes in this typology. So, he just rejected it and eventually, expounded a new theory of utterances, which is known as speech act theory. The speech act theory is considered a *core enterprise* or *a major contribution of Austin*, in the field of analytical philosophy.

Historically, Aristotle was the first philosopher, who distinguished between a sentence and a statement. Whatever we utter, are sentences but not statements. Statements are only those sentences which refer some fact or state of affairs and which are always either true or false. Thus, there are a number of utterances like Questions, Commands, Wishes, Exclamations and so forth which neither indicate some facts nor these are true or false, so that these are not statements. From the philosophical point of view, merely statements are considerable. A statement which does not indicate some fact or state of affairs, is *non-sensical* or *meaningless*. This position was given by logical positivists.

Later on, ordinary language philosophers modified this position and argued that language has not only one job to describe some fact. For example, L. Wittgenstein in his celebrated book, *Philosophical Investigations*, argued for enormous jobs of language, *viz.*, language is not simply assertion of facts or portraying reality but also it is used for asking, thanking, cursing, greeting, praying, commanding, guessing, joking and the like.

J.L. Austin also claimed that there are various uses of language. A number of utterances which are always used to do something rather than or more than used to say something. Let us consider a couple of Austin's example: 'I do this woman my lawful wedded wife', 'I give and bequeath my watch to my brother', 'I bet you six pence it will rain tomorrow', and the like. None of these utterances are true or false, according to Austin. Of course, these are such types of utterances which always perform some acts or stimulate to do some acts. He, therefore, holds that it will be wrong to say that an utterance has only one job to describe some fact and he called it *descriptive fallacy*. As Austin wrote, "We very often also use utterances in ways beyond the scope at least of traditional grammar. It has come to be seen that many specially perplexing words embedded in apparently descriptive statements do not serve to indicate some specially odd additional feature in the reality reported, but to indicate (not to report) to circumstances in which the statement is made or reservations to which it is subject or the way in which it is to be taken and the like. To overlook these possibilities in the way once common is called the *descriptive fallacy*."[1]

In this regard, Austin distinguished utterances into two sorts: the constative and the performative. There are some utterances which must refer some fact, are constative. Whereas some other utterances are always used to operate or act something, are performative. Secondly, the constative utterance is always used to refer to some fact, so that it is always either true or false. The performative utterance does not indicate some fact, but always stimulate to do something. So, it is not true or false, but happy or unhappy. Here, it is important to mention that E.J. Lemmon,[2] in his formulation, *'On Sentences Verifiable by their Use'*, admitted that 'I promise (such and such)' which Austin conceived as performative, is also verifiable by its use and fulfils all those touchstones which are inevitable for a proposition or a statement. Lemmon, therefore, advocated 'I promise (such and such)', as a self-verifiable statement.

Later, Austin pointed some mistakes in this typology and therefore he discarded this distinction and expounded another theory which is known as the speech act theory. According to this theory, *every speech is an act, viz.*, whatever we speak, it not only describes something but also it performs some act. Each utterance, therefore, is used in both the senses; the constative as well as the performative. For example, when a person says "I do you my lawful wedded spouse" then, on the one hand, he accepts someone as his spouse (performs some act), on the other hand, he also describes that I am not already married and if I am married, my wife is not living, sane and the like (which describes something). Similarly, when the Vice-Chancellor of Allahabad University, on the occasion of inaugurating a seminar, asserts that 'I inaugurate this seminar' then he not only inaugurates the seminar but also describes us that he is the chairperson of this seminar.

Later, numerous philosophers like Max Black and R.M. Chisholm endeavoured to justify the above distinction and claimed that Austin's speech act theory hinges upon some fundamental misunderstanding. Max Black in his article, *Austin on performatives*, gave two other definitions of performative utterances. The first, "An utterance is said to be *performative*, when used in specified circumstances, if and only if its being so used counts as a case of the speaker's doing something other than, or something more than, saying something true or false. An utterance that is not performative is called constative."[3] And, the second definition is "An utterance of the form I X (such and such) is said to be *performative*$_B$, when used in a specified circumstances, if and only if its so being is used counts as a case of the speaker's thereby X-ing."[4] Whereas, *X is variable and used for the first person, singular, present, indicative active.*

In both of the definitions, Black advocated the first rather than the second, for happy performatives. The difference between the performative and the constative utterance is *doing* and *saying*. Black conceived that only the first definition fulfils this job, not the second. In this regard, Black showed that there are a number of utterances which are in the form of 'I X such and such', however, which are indeed constative. For instance,

'I state that such and such', which is simply saying something rather than doing something. Moreover, there are a number of utterances which are not in the form of first person, singular, present, indicative, active, in spite of this, these are plainly performative. For example, on the Cricket ground, when an umpire says out! then the term out! does not recite the circumstances. Indeed it performs some act and the player becomes out. Obviously, the term out! is performative and not constative. Black, therefore, advocated that merely first definition deserves for performative, *viz.*, any utterances which form may be anything yet it will be performative, if it is used to do something *inter alia* to say something. As Black wrote, "I am therefore inclined to think that some such notion as that of performative$_A$ will serve the purposes of Austin and all the philosophers who have had high hopes of the notion, and that many if not all of the difficulties that Austin encountered will be overcome by this choice."[5]

L.W. Forguson, in his article, *In pursuit of performative*, criticized Black's definition and assumed that any utterance, even those which are constative (true or false), are also performed some act. Likewise, even those utterances, which are performative, are also true or false. On this account, Austin himself rejected this distinction and emphasized on the *force* of the utterances. For example, *there is a vicious bull in the field*. On the one hand, this utterance recites the situation which can be true or false, like constative. On the other hand, it also performs some other acts. In that sense, it is also performative. For instance, firstly, if you have lost your bull and then by saying this, there is a vicious bull in the field, I inform you. Secondly, suppose your bull is eating my tomato crop and then by saying this, I express my anger. Thirdly, suppose you are about to go in the field and then by saying this, I warn you. Fourthly, if you have seen a strange bull in the field and then by saying this, I express my surprise or error and the like. Thus, there are many dimensions of the language; it can be simply an information, anger, surprise, terror and so forth. So, when we categorise it into two sorts, *i.e.*, the constative and the performative, it is not correct. The nature of utterances is, therefore, determined not only by circumstances but also by the force of utterances, in which an utterance would be used.

Another philosopher R.M. Chisholm also attempted to justify the above distinction, like M. Black. He has determined some characteristics which have shown that why an utterance would be performative. While emphasizing this, Chisholm, firstly distinguished performatives into two sorts—*performative in a strict sense* and *performative in an extended sense*. While defining the performative in a strict sense, he admitted, "There are acts (*e.g.* requesting), which have the following characteristic; when the circumstances are right, then to perform the act it is enough to make certain utterance (*e.g. I request...*) containing an expression which the speaker commonly uses to designate such an act... Let us say, then, of anyone who performs an act in this way, that his utterance is a performative utterance—in a strict sense of this term."[6]

The above definition has shown that an utterance would be performative in the strict sense, if the circumstance is appropriate and then it has always been commonly supported and used to perform some act and which can't be accomplished by some other expressions. For example, *I promise, I request,* etc. When a person utters that 'I promise' then he not only describes about promise but also he does promise and this utterance can't be accomplished by some other ways, like I assurance. Likewise, 'I request', uttered by a person then he does not say something very simply or does not inform about his request, indeed, he does request which can't be replaced by some other expressions and also I request has commonly been used for request, by English speaking man, in the appropriate situation. Hence, Chisholm contended that 'I promise' and 'I request' are performatives in a strict sense.

While defining the performative in an extended sense, Chisholm wrote, "I suggest that the utterance of an expression (*e.g.* I want) is performative in an extended sense of the term, if it is made in order to accomplish that act in virtue of which the utterance of some other expression (*e.g.* request...) can be performative, in the strict sense defined."[7] Thus, an utterance will be performative in the extended sense; firstly, it is not only used to do something but also to say something and secondly, which has always been accomplished by some other expressions. For example, 'I want', 'I know'. 'I want' is performative in the extended sense to the extent that on the one hand, it describes my choice or desire or interest, on the other hand, it also orders the hearer to do something, and which can also be accomplished by some other way like 'I request'. Similarly, 'I know', if a person utters, 'I know' then by saying this he not only describes his psychological state in terms of knowledge but also he gives guarantee about his knowing. Hence, 'I know' may be accomplished by 'I guarantee'. 'I know' is, therefore, concerned with 'I guarantee' whereas 'I want' is related to 'I request'.

Apparently, there are some differences between Austin's and Chisholm's classification. Austin accepted these utterances, *i.e.*, 'I know', and 'I want', as a performative while Chisholm considered it as a performative in the extended sense. According to Austin, 'I want' and 'I know', do not describe any fact or state of affairs while Chisholm argued that these utterances have always been used in both senses; the constative and the performative. Austin's doctrine, therefore, rested upon some mistakes and Chisholm called it *performative fallacy*. As Chisholm wrote, "An utterance of 'I want' may serve both to say something about me and to get you to do something; an utterance of 'I know', similarly, may serve both to say something about me and to provide with guarantees. To suppose that the performative of the latter non-descriptive function is inconsistent with a simultaneous performance of the former, descriptive function, might be called an example of the *performative fallacy*."[8]

L.W. Forguson, however, commented upon Chisholm's formulation. According to him, Chisholm's distinction of performative utterance into the strict sense and the extended sense, could not solve the problems which prevail in Austin's theory. Forguson observed that Chisholm's distinction does not entirely differ from Austin's classification about utterances—*the explicit performative* and *the implicit performative*. Furthermore, he asserted that there may be some utterances, which Austin conceived as performative, however, in the light of Chisholm's definition, these are neither performative in the strict sense nor in the extended sense. For instance, 'I will', when a person utters, 'I will', in the marriage ceremony then he does not describe about the marriage, of course, he accepts someone as his lawful wedded spouse. However, in the light of Chisholm's definitions, this is not performative in the strict sense, if we express it by some other expression like 'I will'. As Forguson argued, ".......the expression 'I will' does not contain a word commonly used by the speaker to designate the act of marrying. Marrying is marrying and not another thing (except perhaps being wed). So, according to Chisholm's definition, 'I will' is not a performative in the strict sense of the term."[9]

'I will' is also not performative in the extended sense, as defined by Chisholm. Forguson argued, there is no other word except 'I will', which is commonly used by the speaker to do this job, in the English speaking world. Hence, 'I will' has commonly been used by the speaker, in the marriage ceremony and which can't accomplish by some other expression (there are no words like, I marry). Hence, it would not be performative, even in the extended sense. While elucidating this Forguson said, "Unfortunately, it is not even a performative in the *extended* sense of the term, as defined by Chisholm. For to utter the expression 'I will' in a marriage ceremony is to accomplish an act (the act of marrying) which could not be accomplished by means of some other expression, the uttering of which in the appropriate circumstances would be performative of marrying in the strict sense of the term. There simply is no expression in English, other than 'I will' (in particular, there is no expression 'I marry......'), the utterance of which in the right circumstances will successfully get one married. And even if there were some other expression that one could utter and thereby marry, it need not be the case that all performative function in this way. It is not difficult to imagine an expression ('I hereby X........') the utterance of which alone can perform some act (the act of Y-ing ), which is never itself used to designate that act; and every word which can be used to designate that act is never used in actual performance of it."[10]

Furthermore, Forguson claimed that in the virtue of Chisholm's definition, an utterance would be performative in the strict sense if and only if it does not accomplish by some other words. However, there are no such words, which can't express by some other expressions. Every word can be replaced by some other ways, according to Forguson. He, therefore, discusses some examples; which are performative in the strict sense, instead these are accomplished by some other ways. For instance, 'I request you to go home', Forguson narrated it in the following ways.

> " 'Oh, why don't you go home?'
> 'Please go home now.'
> 'Don't let me keep you from another engagement.'
> 'It's getting rather late, don't you think?'
> 'I am afraid; I must get up early tomorrow.'
> 'Where has the time gone? And so on.' "[11]

Eventually, Forguson asserted that the distinction between the constative and the performative could not survive. Every utterance has two poles, *viz.*, each utterance has not only been used to do something but also to say something. Forguson, therefore, countenanced Austin's doctrine and also expressed his great disagreement about Black and Chisholm's classification. While emphasizing it, Forguson wrote, "The important point that Austin saw and Chisholm and Black seem to have missed is that there really is no good reason to distinguish between performative and other sorts of utterances at all. All utterances have their performative role to play in discourse: simple assertions as well as promises and requests."[12]

Although, Forguson criticized Chisholm's distinction of performative utterance into the strict sense and the extended sense. However, when we subtly examine Forguson's argument, we can show that his contention underpinned over some *logical contradiction.* For instance, Forguson conceived that 'I will' is neither performative in the strict sense nor in the extended sense, in the light of Chisholm's definition. It is not performative in the strict sense inasmuch as marrying is marrying and not another thing. So, when we express it by

'I will', of course, it would not be performative in the strict sense. It is also not performative in the extended sense to the extent that there is no any alternative word *vis-à-vis* 'I will' for marriage in the English speaking world.

Forguson, however, missed an important point, if marriage is expressed by some other expression like 'I will'. Indeed, it will be performative in the strict sense to the extent that Forguson himself asserted that there is no any other word (like I marry), rather than 'I will' for marriage, in the English speaking world. It is also performative in the extended sense inasmuch as marrying is marrying and not the other thing. So, if it is expressed by some other expression like 'I will', it must be performative in the extended sense. This discussion delineates that 'I will' could be performative in the both senses: the strict and the extended.

Furthermore, Forguson argued that an utterance has many dimensions like, it can be an order, a warning, an advice, a surprise, a terror and so forth. However, we may consider some utterances, as plainly constative, not performative. Suppose, Ram and Shyam both have Santro cars and in their discussion, Ram asserts to Shyam that Santro's performance is better than other cars. Here, Ram does not advice Shyam to purchase the Santro car. He simply gives an information about Santro car. The utterance is, therefore, constative and not performative. Likewise, a number of utterances are used merely in the descriptive sense. For example, descartes was the father of the modern western philosophy. Atom is the simplest form of matter. There is Tajmahal in Agra. Allahabad fort was constructed by Akbar. Birbal was the chief advisor of Akbar. Lord Buddha was the founder of Buddhism. Delhi is the capital of India. Calcutta was the capital of India before 1911. Prof. A.C. Mukharjee was the former Head of the Department of philosophy, Allahabad University. Sāṁkhya philosophy is one of the oldest philosophy in India. Mount Everest is one of the highest mountains of the world. Ved Vyas was the author of *Mahabharat*. Harvard University is located in U.S.A. Of course, these utterances do not perform acts, except they give some information. So, these are merely constative and not performative.

Over and above, there may be some utterances with many dimensions. However, all the dimensions of an utterance are not possible at a time and at a place. *If all the dimensions of an utterance would be possible at a time, and at a place, then the question of indeterminacy of meaning must emerge*. Of course, an utterance is used in various contexts and according to contexts, it acquires varied meanings. However, merely context is not adequate for clarification of the meaning. There are several cases, where contexts do not clarify the accurate meaning of utterances. For example, *Saindhava*, the Hindi word *Saindhava* means both salt and horse. When a solider exclaimed *Saindhava* in the war field, its meaning would be horse, not salt. While, a person used the same word on the dining table, its meaning would be salt, not horse. Instead, we may consider this problem in some other way. Suppose, I am on the dining table and eating food. In the meantime, someone has come and informed me that enemies are about to attack you. While hearing this, I just exclaimed *Saindhava*. Of course, its meaning would be horse, not salt. The context of the dining table physically doesn't change but utterance like 'enemies are about to attack' changes the real meaning of the context. Thus, the context is dynamic in nature.

This problem compels us to reconsider about the issue that: *whether the contextual theory is adequate?* In the light of the above discussion, we may say that *the contextual meaning is not enough to know the actual meaning of any word*. There may be some circumstances, where the speaker's intention is much more important than the context. By and large, when a speaker used any word, we avoid or ignore his intention (which is subjective) and according to the context (which is objective), we judge the meaning which may not be correct or appropriate. In spite of this, there may be possible some contexts, where, speaker's intention performs major role. Therefore, it is convincingly argued that there are two things, which are very important for the clarification of the meaning of an utterance: the first, *contexts or circumstances* and the second, *the speaker's intentions*.

Although, Prof. R. Prasad, in his article, *A functional Analysis of Language*, used context in very board sense which has contained numerous factors. As he wrote, "A context of use is a very complex thing, which contains human as well as non-human factors. In brief, it consists of the intentions, attitudes, etc., of the speaker, the intonation of the utterance, its effects (intended, expected, or actual) on the hearer, the psychological state of the hearer, the relation of the speaker to the hearer, the occasion of use, the physical conditions prevailing at the time, etc."[13] However, Prasad's view was not accepted by most of the philosophers. Even, Wittgenstein used this word only in the objective sense, not in the subjective sense. If we subtly consider this problem, we will have to distinguish the subjective and the objective criteria.

While elaborating the nature of meaning, I.A. Richard[14] in his article, *The four kinds of Meaning*, conceived four possible meanings of an utterance:

- Sense meaning
- Feeling meaning
- Tone meaning
- Intention meaning

Precisely, out of these four meanings, sense meaning, tone meaning, and intention meaning are concerned with the speaker, while the feeling meaning is concerned with the hearer. It quite likely implies that while deducing the meaning of an utterance, one must emphasize on both of facets, the speaker as well as the hearer.

In this regard, we can plainly distinguish between the constative and the performative utterances. A speaker does not always use a word for doing something. Sometimes a speaker simply wants to inform the hearer, *viz.*, he would like to give some information. For example, if a father tells his son that Atal Bihari Bajpayee is the Prime Minister of India, this utterance may be stimulation, or an instruction or simply information. The question is: what is the real intention of the speaker? If the father simply gives an information to his son then it will be constative, otherwise it will be performative to the extent that it is also possible that father would like to stimulate his son that your character and your works should be like Atal Bihari Bajpayee. If we ignore speaker's intention, we will not be able to judge the actual meaning of this utterance. *Thus, the intention of the speaker is critically important in understanding the meaning of utterances. Merely knowledge of context in which an utterance takes place may not be adequate in understanding the meaning assigned by the speaker. The hearer also attempts to make inference regarding intention of the speaker.*

In the light of above discussion, we may consider Forguson's example, *there is a vicious bull in the field*. Indeed, this utterance can be an information, an order, an anger, or surprise, terror, etc., however, all the possible senses are not appropriate at a time and at a place. It may vary due to variations of time and place and its meaning not only underpinned over context but also on the *speaker's intentions*. Thus, in the virtue of *the primary of the purposes or purposes of use*, it can be plainly shown that the distinction between the constative and the performative is justifiable. If we avoid this, it would raise *controversy of unavoidable nature*.

## REFERENCES

1. Austin, J.L. (1980): *How to Do Things with Words*, J.O. Urmson and M. Sbisa (Ed.), p. 3.
2. Lemmon, E.J. (1962): *On Sentences Verifiable by their Use Analysis*, Vol. 22, No. 4. pp. 86-89.
3. Black, M (1969): *Austin On Performatives*, In K. Fann (Ed.) Symposium On J.L. Austin, pp. 403-404.
4. *Ibid.* p. 405.
5. *Ibid.* p. 406.
6. Chisholm, R.M. (1969): *Austin's Philosophical Papers*. In K.T. Fann (Ed.) Symposium on J.L. Austin pp. 109-10.
7. *Ibid.* p. 110.
8. *Ibid.* p. 111.
9. Forguson, L.W. (1969): *In Pursuit of Performative*. In K.T. Fann (Ed.) Symposium on J.L. Austin p. 415.
10. *Ibid.* p. 415.
11. *Ibid.* p. 416.
12. *Ibid.* p. 419.
13. Prasad, R. (1989): *Regularity, Normativity And Rules of Language and Other Essays in Philosophical Analysis*, p. 3.
14. Richard, I.A. in his article, *The four kinds of Meaning*. Edited in David Lodge (1972): "20th Century Literary Criticism", p. 116.

# 5

# Speech Act Theory

Invitation to William James lecture series at Harvard University in 1955 provided an opportunity to J.L. Austin for presenting his discourse on speech act theory. In his lectures, Austin synthesized his seminal ideas to disseminate the ultimate form of his theory to the academic world.

In his classic book, *How to Do Things with Words,* Austin distinguished between the constative and the performative utterances. The constative means description or information, which is true or false. The performance, however, means an action or an instruction or stimulation to do something like promise, order and so forth. Thus, these are not true or false, but solely happy and unhappy. Later, Austin himself felt that this distinction was awry. He, therefore, modified this distinction and argued that *every speech is an act,* which is known as speech act theory. This theory advocates, "The total speech act in the total speech-situation".[1] Walter Cert called it *core enterprises*[2] of 'How to Do Things with Words'.

Austin classified speech act into: Locutionary, Illocutionary and Perlocutionary acts. The locutionary act is an act of saying something in the full normal sense. When we say something in the full normal sense, it incorporates the utterance of certain noises; the utterance of grammatically correct vocables and the utterance of some certain sense and reference. Austin, therefore, introduced the concepts of the phonetic, the phatic and the rhetic act, respectively. "The phonetic act is merely the act of uttering certain noises. The phatic act is the uttering of certain vocables or words, *i.e.,* noises of certain types, belonging to and as belonging to, a certain vocabulary, conforming to and as conforming to, a certain grammar. The rhetic act is the performance of an act of using those vocables with a certain more-or-less definite sense and reference."[3]

Although, all these three acts are indispensable for locutionary act, however, the phatic and the rhetic act are more complicated. Austin conceived that three things are *sine qua non* for the phatic act; a certain vocabulary—words or phrases; it should be with appropriate intonation; and it must confirmed to certain grammar. Thus, the phatic act comprises, "......the intonation as well as grammar and vocabulary."[4] Anyone of mistakes in the above conditions may be fallacious which he called *nonsense or meaningless*. "The pheme is a unit of language: its typical fault is to be nonsense—meaningless."[5]

In all likelihood, we may fulfil these conditions without knowing its meaning, *i.e., sense* and *reference*. In the childhood, for instance, we were mimicking a poem without knowing its meaning. It reveals that the knowledge of sense and reference is essential for successful performance. While distinguishing the sense and reference, he divided two sorts of conventions; *convention of sense* and *convention of reference*, which he called *descriptive conventions* and *demonstrative conventions* respectively. The former is concerned with speaker's meaning, while the later is concerned with historic situation. "*Descriptive* conventions correlating the words (sentences) with the *types* of situation, thing, event, & C., to be found in world (statements). *Demonstrative* conventions correclating the words with the *historic* situations, & C, to be found in the world."[6]

The *sense* of the word insinuates the speaker's meaning. G.J. Warnock writes, "As to 'sense', we need to grasp not only what the words used mean—or the several things they *could* mean—in the language; we need to grasp what the speaker meant by those words (what he used them *as* meaning) in the particular case."[7] For instance, 'The case is closed.' This utterance has two different meanings. On the one, its meaning may be a certain item of luggage is closed in the suitcase, on the other, it also suggests that the certain legal proceeding has come to an end. The *sense* of the word is, however, that meaning which the speaker comprehends and conceives, so that it is underpinned upon the speaker's meaning.

The *reference* of the word is concerned with its historic situation. "In order to know 'what he said' in saying that 'the case was closed', we need to know not only what he meant by *case* and *closed*, and not only what case, or which case, he was referring to, but, rather roughly, which case when: we need to identify the 'historic situation' which, in speaking as he did, he intended to report or describe."[8] The knowledge of sense and reference of a sentence is, therefore, indispensable for the elucidation of meaning, which Austin called the *rhetic act*. If we fault any of the foresaid condition, some ambiguity would be emerged, which he called vague or void or obscure. ".......the rheme is a unit of speech; its typical fault is to be vague or void or obscure, & C."[9]

Austin, moreover, delineates the relation among all the three acts; the phonetic act, the phatic act, and the rhetic act.[10] Albeit, all of the three are indispensable for the locutionary act, nonetheless these are separable as well as distinguishable from each other. When we utter the phatic act, for instance, it also implies the phonetic act to the extent that when we utter something which is grammatically correct, it also subsumes some certain noises. However, the phonetic *i.e.*, merely certain noise does not contain the phatic act *i.e.*, grammatically correct vocables. Likewise, when we utter the rhetic act, it must be the phatic act, but the phatic acts doesn't contain the rhetic acts. Apparently, the rhetic act is bound up with sense and reference, so that when we utter the rhetic act it will be certainly comprised grammatically correct vocables. Whereas, the grammatically correct vocables *e.g.*, mimicking a poem may not necessarily underlie certain sense and reference. Moreover, the phatic acts may be direct, while the rhetic acts may be indirect. Hence, all the three acts the phonetic, the phatic and the rhetic act are different to each other. "The act of saying something in the full normal sense, I call, *i.e.*, dub, the performance of a locutionary act......"[11]

Walter Cerf, in his article, *Critical Review of How to Do Things with Words*, raises numerous questions regarding the phonetic, the phatic and the rhetic act. He argues that Austin classifies speech act into locutionary, illocutionary, and perlocutionary act. Again, the locutionary act is classified into the phonetic, the phatic and the rhetic act. These are subclasses within the locutionary act. However, there is a close connectivity among them. For instance, we can make certain noises without uttering words but not *vice versa*. Likewise, we can utter words, which have no meaning, while meaning can't be convey without words. Thus, all the three acts are not the subclass of locutionary act, but these are composite ingredients of locutionary act. As Cerf wrote, "The suspicion arises that the phonetic act, the phatic act and the rhetic act are not subclass, but parts of the locutionary act—as blossom, stem, leaf and root are parts and not classes of flowers.... They all have together if a locutionary act is come off."[12] He, further, argues that Austin himself accepts, "......the phatic act, the phonetic act and the rhetic act, etc., are mere abstraction."[13] If it is correct then why Austin called them *act*? While commenting upon these acts, Cerf says, "But if phonetic, phatic and rhetic acts are mere aspects of locutionary act, why call them acts? Surely, the red of the rose will be a flower only to one who does not know how to use flower."[14]

Well, Cerf rightly says that the phonetic, the phatic and the rhetic act are composite parts of locutionary act. Hence, these can't be subclass within locutionary act. In addition, it can't be even *act* inasmuch as their existence is not separate from locutionary act. However, when we subtly observe, we may say that Austin used the term *act* in very broad sense. Any sort of sound which performs any kind of action must be known as act. In this regard, merely locutionary act can't be act. Even the phonetic act, the phatic and the rhetic act are also called as *act*. The phonetic act means a certain sound without sense and reference. However, we should not forget that a certain sound may perform some act. Let me suppose that a person is merely crying. This sound, however, may perform some act by creating some hurdle to others or it may be an indication of something. In such a situation it must be treated as an *act*. Likewise, the phatic act must be *act* to the extent that grammatically correct vocables without knowing its real sense and reference may be important from hearer's point of view. In this regard, it may perform some act and thereby it may be meaningful. Finally, there is no doubt about the rhetic act. It is necessarily concerned with certain sense and reference. So far as, I understand, by virtue of this, Austin called them acts.

Apart from, it seems that these are not only composite part of locutionary act but these acts have independent entity from locutionary act. Indeed, these are separable as well as distinguishable also. The phonetic act doesn't contain the phatic act. Likewise, the phatic act doesn't comprise the rhetic act. Thus, these are separate from each other. On this account, in all likelihood, it may be subclass within locutionary act.

G.J. Warnock also comments upon that when Austin classified varied sort of acts, like the phonetic, the phatic and the rhetic along with the locutionary, the illocutionary and the perlocutionary acts, he endeavours to fuse two different sorts of languages; *Greek based language* and *Latin based language*. While, in the real sense, there is no distinction between the rhetic act and the locutionary act to the extent that both are concerned with certain *sense* and *reference*. For instance, locutionary act is an act of saying something in the full normal sense. When we say something in the full normal sense, it underlies certain sense and reference. It is on the par with the rhetic act inasmuch as it also emphasises on certain sense and reference. In that sense, both are similar to each other in terms of sense and reference. The only difference is; one is Latin-based language, while, the other is Greek-based language. "It looks to me as if 'locutionary act' is a Latin-based and the 'rhetic act' a Greek-based, name for exactly the same thing...... If we start with the Greek term 'phonetic', and go on to 'phatic', it is natural to round off, so to speak, that particular trait with another Greek-based level, 'rhetic'. If we work backwards from the Latinate 'perlocutionary act' to the Latinate 'illocutionary act', it is natural to fill out that triad with an appropriate Latin-based level, 'locutionary'. Austin may just not have noticed—certainly he nowhere says explicitly—what it take to be case, that in fact we have a sort of overlap here, with one Greek and one Latin label for just the same thing the Greek label looking backwards, so to speak, to 'phatic' and 'phonetic', and the Latin label forwards, to 'illocution' and 'perlocution'."[15]

Precisely, at the surface, it seems that there is no distinction between the locutionary act and the phatic act. The only difference is that one is Greek-based language and the other is Latin-based. However, close in depth study of the whole episode reveals that this distinction is justifiable. When Austin classifies locutionary act into the phonetic, the phatic and the rhetic act, this is one level of distinction which hinges upon 'the form of language.' It is indispensable for meaningful expression. If we want to successfully communicate something in language, we must follow these paces. In this regard, these three acts are closely connected to each other. In addition, when Austin classifies acts into locutionary, illocutionary and perlocutionary, this distinction relies upon other level which is bound up with the 'use and its function of language'. It advocates many functions of language. In that sense, both are different to each other. Apart from, let me suppose that the locutionary and the rhetic act are similar to each other in terms of sense and reference. In spite of this both are different. When Austin distinguishes the locutionary act, he goes on the phonetic, the phatic, and the rhetic act. But when he distinguishes the function of language, he goes on to the locutionary, the illocutionary and the perlocutionary act. I, therefore, may say that both of the distinctions are justifiable inasmuch as both perform two different purposes.

Over and above, Austin averred that while performing a locutionary act, we also perform an illocutionary act, *viz.*, of saying something; we must perform some other acts like, insinuating, arguing, warning, criticizing, stimulating, etc. All these acts are known as illocutionary acts. As Austin says:

> "Asking or answering a question,
> Giving some information or an assurance or a warning,
> Announcing a verdict or an intention,
> Pronouncing sentence,
> Making an appointment or an appeal or a criticism,
> Making an identification or giving a description, and the numerous like."[16]

Austin asserts that we may use our utterances in numerous ways, which he calls the illocutionary act. "......to determine what illocutionary act is......we must determine in what way we are using the location."[17] It accentuates that we may use our utterances in varied ways, like describing, advising, warning and so forth, which has decided the *force* of utterance. Indeed, each utterance has some certain force to do something, Austin calls it illocutionary force. Thus, illocutionary act is an act, which we perform in saying something. When we say something in the full normal sense (locutionary act), in saying something we also perform some other acts like, alarming, advising, etc., (illocutionary act). Austin, therefore, distinguishes between *meaning* and *force* in the light of locutionary and illocutionary act. This contribution of Austin has enriched analytical philosophy significantly. Prior to Austin, by and large, this distinction was ignored by philosophers. As Austin contended, "......performance of an act *in saying* something as opposed to performance of an act *of saying* something; I call the act performed an 'illocution' and shall refer to the doctrine of the different types of function of language here in question as the doctrine of *'illocutionary force'*. It may be said that for too long philosophers have neglected this study, treating all problems as problems of 'illocutionary usage'...... But I want to distinguish force and meaning in the sense in which meaning is equivalent to sense and reference......"[18]

Walter Cerf remarks that this is not entirely a new conception in Austin's philosophy. When Austin distinguishes between the constative and the performative utterance, he has already accepted this distinction. "This doctrine is Aufbebung of his old distinction between performatives and constatives. The old distinction is being observed by a new one; that between the force and the meaning of an utterance. The doctrine of speech acts classifies the forces of an utterance."[19]

He, therefore, distinguishes between the locutionary act and the illocutionary act in the light of meaning and force.

- On the one, locutionary act is bound up with its literal meaning; on the other, illocutionary act is bound up with force. Albeit, a word or a sentence has definite meaning nonetheless regarding the force, its meaning may vary.

- Locutionary act is topic-oriented, while illocutionary act is audience-directed.[20]
- Illocutionary act but not locutionary act is conventional. "We must notice that the illocutionary act is a conventional act; an act done as conforming to a convention."[21]
- Locutionary act may not be intentional, while, illocutionary act is always intentional. "....the illocutionary act can't be unintentionally performed."[22]
- Locutionary act is concerned with language, whereas, illocutionary act is concerned with speech. "The illocutionary dimension is, therefore, more concerned with speech than with language."[23]

Austin, furthermore, pretends that while performing a locutionary act and therein an illocutionary act, we also perform some other acts, which he called *perlocutionary act*. For instance, by saying something we may achieve some consequential effects on the feelings, thoughts, actions and decisions of the hearers. As he said, "Saying something will often, or even normally, produce certain consequential effects upon the feelings, thoughts, or actions of the audience, or of the speaker, or of the other person."[24] Plainly, by telling something to someone, one may change his opinion on some issues or mislead him or surprise him or persuade him or stimulate him to do or not to do something and so forth. Perlocutionary act is, therefore, bound up with its consequences, *viz.*, what effect we impose on the feeling and thought of the hearer or *what I did*. By telling him as to *my horse is not fully fit*, for instance, I can change his opinion for not to purchase this horse or instruct him not to use this horse for racing or also give him advice to keep away from this horse inasmuch as this horse is vicious or dull and so on and so forth.

Warnock points out three important characteristics of perlocutionary act. "First, it is, as we shall see, important that the production of such effects may or may not be intended by the performer, and may not occur even if he intends that it should—I may perlocutionary shock you unintentionally by making what I take to be some quite innocent remark, or alternatively may fail to shock you when that is my intention. Second, the perlocutionary effect in question will very often be producible also in some completely *non-verbal* way—I may deter you from betting on my horse not by saying anything but by knocking you down, or may shock you by lighting a cigarette in church, but it is clearly intended that such effects come into—or can be said to be—the performance of *real* perlocutionary acts only when they are brought about by *saying* something. And third, it is I think at least implicit in what Austin says that, for a perlocutionary act to be performed, the effects in question must be effects of (at least) a full *locutionary act*. I might startle you, for example, by the phonetic act of speaking loudly in your ear, or (if I have been thought hitherto to be hopeless aphasic) by the phatic act of saying anything at all; but it seems to be part of the notion of a perlocutionary act that the effect in the question is brought about by my *saying what I say*, not merely by my speaking at all, or saying anything at all."[25]

Austin further distinguishes between the illocutionary and the perlocutionary act. Firstly, the illocutionary act is a matter of *what I mean*, whereas, perlocutionary act is a matter of *what actually happened*. While elucidating this Keith Graham says, "......for the successful performance of any perlocutionary act it will be necessary that some consequential change occur in the attitudes, beliefs or actions or one's audience; whereas for the successful performance of an illocutionary act all that need occur beyond the utterance itself is that the audience understand it."[26]

Secondly, illocutionary acts are conventional, while perlocutionary act may not be conventional. "Speaking of the use of 'language' for arguing or warning, looks just like speaking of 'the use of 'language' for persuading, rousing alarming, yet the former may, for contrast, be said to be conventional,...... But the later could not.[27] Again, "Illocutionary acts are conventional acts: perlocutionary are not conventional."[28] Furthermore, "Strictly speaking, there can't be an illocutionary act unless the means employed are conventional."[29] Moreover, "...... we also perform illocutionary acts such as informing, ordering, warning, undertaking, etc., *i.e.*, utterances which have a certain (conventional) force."[30]

Thirdly, illocutionary act may be non-verbal. It does not mean that it is not conventional. A non-verbal illocutionary act must be conventional but perlocutionary act are not conventional. "Acts of both kinds can be performed—or, more accurately, acts called by the same name (for example, acts equivalents to the illocutionary act or warning or the perlocutionary act or convincing)—can be brought off non-verbally; but even then to deserve the name of illocutionary act, for example, a warning, it must be a conventional non-verbal act."[31]

Fourthly, illocutionary acts are intentional, while perlocutionary acts are not intentional. Austin thinks that for the successful perlocutionary act, it is indispensable that the hearer must grasp the speaker's intention. The hearer sometimes may fail to grasp the very intention of the speaker. On this account, Austin emphasises that the hearer must recognize the speaker's intention. Thus, there are two things for illocutionary acts: *it must be intentional* and also *it should be uptake and recognized by the hearer*. Warnock writes, "There are two points to be made. First, the perlocutionary act—any such act—may be performed unintentionally; ......It seems right to say, by contrast, that the illocutionary act can't be unintentionally performed ......Second, it is I think a more substantial point that the illocutionary intention, if we call it that, unlike the perlocutionary intention, is actually fulfilled on the sole condition that it is recognized."[32]

M. Furberg, in his article *Meaning and Illocutionary Force*, admitted two specific characteristics of illocutionary act which differentiates it from perlocutionary act. "(1) They are conventional—done as conforming to a convention. (2) They are up to the speaker, in the sense that their successful performance does not demand any response from the audience other than a mere understanding of their convention—governed force. In both these respects they resemble locutionary acts and differ from perlocutionary ones."[33]

While distinguishing between illocutionary and perlocutionary act, W.P. Alston highlights three points, "(1) As already noted, perlocutionary, but not illocutionary acts, essentially involve the production of some effect...... (2) An illocutionary act, unlike the perlocutionary act, requires a locutionary act as a base...... I can get you to pass the salt by simply looking around for it... (3) Another noteworthy difference between the two categories is that an illocutionary act can be means to a perlocutionary act, but not *vice versa.* I can request that you pass the salt in order to get you to pass the salt."[34]

Austin himself conceives that "......the illocutionary act is distinct from perlocutionary act is connected with the production of the effects in certain senses.

- ...... the performance of an illocutionary act involves the *securing of uptake.*
- The illocutionary act *takes effect* in a certain ways, as distinguished from producing consequences in the sense of bringing about states of affairs in the *normal* way, *i.e.*, changes in the natural course of events......
- ......numerous illocutionary acts invite by convention a response or sequel......

So here three ways in which illocutionary acts are bound up with effects; and these are all distinct from the producing of effects which is the characteristic of the perlocutionary act."[35]

Austin, therefore, differentiates the locutionary, the illocutionary and the perlocutionary acts in the following ways: The locutionary act, *he said that* '......', the illocutionary act, *he argued that* '.....', and the perlocutionary act, *he convinced me* that '.....'. For instance, *of saying* that 'my horse is not fully fit' (locutionary act); *in saying* this 'I give you a warning' (illocutionary act); and *by saying* this 'I may succeed to change your position *i.e.*, you don't purchase this horse (perlocutionary act). Hence, the locutionary act is an act *of saying* something; the illocutionary act is an act of *in saying* something, whereas, the perlocutionary act is an act of *by saying*, something.

In the course of time, Austin highlighted the illocutionary act and thus the locutionary act and the perlocutionary act gradually faded away. As Austin wrote, "Our interest in these lectures is essentially to fasten on the second, illocutionary act and contrast it with the other two."[36] For the illocutionary act, Austin emphasised on the *securing uptake, i.e.,* the hearer must understand the meaning as well as force of the utterance. In all likelihood, the hearer may fail to grasp the force of the utterance, whatever the speaker would like to communicate. By virtue of this, Austin concluded that the hearer must recognize speaker's intention, otherwise the utterance would be infelicitous. He, therefore, pointed out two characteristics for successful illocutionary act: the first, it must be *conventional* and the second, *it should be grasped and recognized by the hearer*. "Unless a certain effect is achieved, the illocutionary act will not have been happily, successfully performed...... Generally the effect amounts to bringing about the understanding of the meaning and of the force of the locution. So, the performance of an illocutionary act involves the *"securing uptake."*[37]

In the penultimate chapter of his book *How to Do Things with Words*, Austin reviewed the distinction of the constative and the performative utterance. In this regard, he raised some pertinent questions about the performative and the constative utterances. Firstly, can we say that there is a special class of utterances, to be called performatives which is always used to do something rather than to say something, unlike the constative utterance? And, secondly, may we say that the form of performatives are felicitous or infelicitous, whereas, the form of the constatives are true or false. Although, at the outset of his book, Austin advocated this distinction, but now he observes some inconsistency in this typology. So, he discarded it, basically on two counts.

Firstly, there is no demarcation line between *doing* and *saying*. When we say something, it also entails to do something, *viz.*, to say something is always concerned with to do something. Each locutionary act is, therefore, bound up with illocutionary acts, and eventually it is concerned with perlocutionary acts. Thus, the distinction between doing and saying or we may say the performative and the constative could not sustain for long. Austin himself remarks, "Surely to state is every bit as much to perform an illocutionary act as, say, to warn or to pronounce.....

Stating seems to meet all the criteria we had for distinguishing the illocutionary act..... Stating is put absolutely on a level with arguing, betting, and warning."[38] For instance, 'In saying that it is raining,' it may be betting, warning, and so forth. Likewise, 'I state that he did not do it.' It may be simply an information or it may be a kind of argument. The distinction between saying and doing is, therefore, not appropriate.

Secondly, Austin asserted that it is alright that a statement is in the form of true or false. It does not mean that it may not be happy or unhappy. Indeed, it may also be happy or unhappy, like performative utterance. For example, when I state that I sell you something, which is not mine or when I state something which I do not believe. Or, when I state that my car is in the garage, whereas I have no car or probably no garage. In such a situation, this utterance will not be false but simply unhappy. Thus, the constative utterance may be happy and unhappy, like the performative.

Later on, Austin argued that although, saying is concerned with illocutionary act which may be happy or unhappy. In spite of this, the constative contains some specific quality. By and large, the form of the constative utterance is either true or false. But, when we valuate this utterance on the certain grounds, it may be in some other forms, like right or wrong, correct or incorrect and so forth. "We may feel that here is a dimension in which we judge, assess, or appraise the constative utterance (granting as a preliminary that it is felicitous) which does not arise with non-constative or performative utterance."[39]

By virtue of this, Austin tried to prove that there is an alternation in the constative utterance. It proceeds towards truth or falsity, to right or wrong, correct or incorrect. As he wrote, "....... there is an obvious slide towards truth or falsity in the case of, for example verdictives, such as estimating, finding and pronouncing."[40] For instance, we may infer that it is half past two rightly or wrongly; we may find that he is guilty, correctly or incorrectly as well as we may pronounce that the batsman is out correctly or incorrectly. Thus, truth or falsity is sliding towards right or wrong, correct or incorrect and the like.

Warnock expressed his dissatisfaction about Austin's contention and argued that there is indeed a gap in this doctrine. In his words, "My reason for saying that the point is understated is this: that in these other cases we surely have, not really a slide towards truth or falsity, but involvement of the very same notion of truth and falsity as in the case of statements."[41] For instance, 'In saying that it is raining.' I am not betting, arguing, or warning. I am simply stating or describing a fact. Moreover, he assumes that if stating is equivalent to arguing, betting, or warning, then 'In saying that it is raining,' I am arguing or betting or warning. And then what is the common factor in these utterances? Plainly, the common factor is, 'It is raining.' Of course, this is a statement which will be factually correct. Similarly, when 'I say that it is half past two', if it is true, then I am making an estimate, my estimate will be right. Or, when 'I say that he is guilty', if this is true, then I am giving a verdict, my verdict will be correct. By virtue of this, Warnock attempted to prove that the fundamental characteristic of the constative utterance, *e.g.*, truth or falsity, is unalterable, so that it will be wrong to say that there is 'sliding' involved in the constative utterance.

To enforce the above view, Austin criticised the varied theories of 'truth', like the correspondence theory of truth, and the pragmatic theory of truth. The correspondence theory of truth begins with Socrates' philosophy. This theory advocates that a statement or an idea will be true, if there will be a corresponding fact in accordance with the statement or the idea. While commenting upon this doctrine, Austin argued that there are numerous statements which have no corresponding facts. Instead, these are not false. For example, 'France is hexagonal', by and large, it is true but it is not correct, for a geographer. Similarly, 'All snow geese migrate to Labrador.' In case, a maim geese could not migrate to Labrador, due to his disability. May I say that the above statement is false. Likewise, suppose that a person says that 'all swans are white.' In the course of time, if we found a black swan, may I say that this statement became false? Of course, even in that condition this statement will not be absolutely false. The person, therefore, may argue that I was not talking about all swans absolutely everywhere and in all times. Indeed, 'Reference' depends on knowledge at the time of utterance."[42]

The above discussion highlights the fact that the truth of a statement underpins over the circumstances or situations in which an utterance takes place. Apparently, this doctrine is far from the logical analysis of the truth. As he wrote, "In real life, as opposed to the simple situations envisaged in logical theory, one cannot always answer in a simple manner whether is it true or false."[43]

When Austin argues that the truth of a statement not only hinges upon its corresponding fact but also on the circumstances in which the statement is used, it doesn't mean that this theory of truth is concerned with the pragmatic theory of truth. Here, it is important to mention that the pragmatic theory of truth advocates that *truth hinges upon its practical importance or utility*. A statement or an idea will be true, if it is useful. And the thing which will be useful must be true. Hence, truth and usefulness are synonymous to each other. So far as Austin is concerned, he clearly distinguished between the pragmatic theory and his own theory of truth. Austin advocates that the truth of a statement underpins over the circumstances or situations, in which the statement is used and thereby he doesn't emphasize on the practical consequences. As he wrote, "It is essential to realize that 'true' and 'false', like 'free' or 'unfree', do not stand for anything simple at all; but only for a general dimension of being a right or proper thing to say as opposed to a wrong thing, in these circumstances, to this audience, for these purposes and with these intentions..... This doctrine is quite different from that pragmatists have said, to the effect that the true is what works & C. The truth or falsity of a statement depends not merely on the meanings of the words but on what act you were performing in what circumstances."[44] Apparently, Austin emphasised on the circumstances or situations *inter alia* corresponding fact or practical consequences. On this account, Austin argued in favour of the *total speech-act in the total speech-situation*. "The total speech act in the total speech-situation is the only actual phenomenon which in the last resort, we are engaged in elucidating."[45]

In the final chapter, Austin distinguishes the speech-act into 'five very general classes,' but he is not equally happy about all of them and also doesn't pay much attention to this classification. He himself believed that this is the matter of 'prolonged fieldwork.' So, he points out merely examples of this classes. As he himself holds, "I shall only give you a run around, or rather a flounder around."[46] These five classes are followings:

(i) Verdictives
(ii) Exercitives
(iii) Commissives
(iv) Behabitives
(v) Expositives

While elaborating this Austin writes, "The first, verdictives are typified by the giving of a verdict, as the name implies, by a jury, arbitrator, or an umpire. But they need not be final; they may be, for example, an estimate, reckoning, or appraisal....... The second, exercitives are the exercising of powers, rights or influence. Examples are. appointing, voting, ordering, urging, advising warning & C. The third, commissives are typified by promising or otherwise undertaking; they commit you to doing something, but included also declarations or announcements of intention, which are not promises, and also rather vague things which we may call espousals, as for example, siding with...... The fourth, behabitives are a very miscellaneous group, and have to do with attitudes and social behaviour. Examples are apologizing, congratulating, commending, condoling, cursing, and challenging. The fifth, expositives are difficult to define. They make plain, how are our utterances fit into the course of an argument, conversation, how we are using words, or in general, are expository. Examples are I reply, I argue, I concede, I illustrate, I assume, I postulate."[47]

Later, a number of distinguished philosophers like, Walter Cerf, P.F. Strawson, L.J. Cohen, Mats Furberg, John Searle, Charles Travis, L.W. Forguson, David Hold Craft, G.J. Warnock and many others criticised as well as proposed revisions through their formulations. Cerf subtly evaluates all the aspects of speech act theory and expresses his dissatisfaction about Austin's classification of speech act into locutionary, illocutionary, and perlocutionary act. According to Cerf, these are not the classification of speech act but are simply the composite parts of the speech act. The classification of speech act into locutionary, illocutionary, and perlocutionary acts is, therefore, preposterous. For instance, if a patient shouts Ouch! on the dentist chair, then he not only expresses his pain, but also he is giving a warning to dentist. Hence, every speech is an act. Cerf further argues that even Austin himself concedes this, when he said, "The locutionary as much as the illocutionary is an abstraction only. Every genuine speech act is both."[48]

Cerf also makes a further observation that speech act or performance of speech act is an unfortunate choice of Austin. Actually, these terms have always been used in the circus and varied other shows like drama, cinema, and the like. These are never used in our daily life. As he asserted, "It must be observed, first of all, that, as an ordinary phrase of everyday discourse, 'performing an act' is of a rather limited use. In fact, the only context in which 'performing an act' sounds quite ordinary is the somewhat extraordinary world of the circus and variety shows in a less dramatic way, someone is said to be performing an act when he is doing things as if he were on the stage."[49]

Over and above, Cerf commented that although Austin set up his goal to elucidate 'the total speech-act in the total speech situation,' but he was unable to achieve this goal. Of course, the word 'total' is very wide term, which is not only used in philosophy but also it is used in numerous other disciplines, like sociology, psychology, and so forth. Hence, in the view of Cerf the term 'total' is not the appropriate. In his words, "The total speech act is meant to be the speech act considered in all its aspects, or at least in all its essential aspects, and not in just one or some;... Yet, this total speech act is surely too much for any philosopher to bite off. There are aspects of the speech act and that is interesting to the sociologist, others to the psychologist, others again to the communications technician, and so on. Are philosopher supposed to be interested in all of these, synthesizing them into an overall theory?"[50] Cerf, therefore, attempted to show that Austin's elucidation of 'the total speech-act in the total speech situation' is far from linguistic analysis and bound up with an existential analysis. As he said, ".....his elucidation was a step away from linguistic analysis, he surely was in no way aware of having moved, ever so modestly, towards an existential analysis of sorts."[51]

In his article, *Intention and Convention in Speech Acts*, P.F. Strawson also criticised Austin's speech act theory. Strawson states that for illocutionary act, Austin emphasised on notably two things; firstly, *convention* and secondly, *securing of uptake*. But, Austin could not justify his claims. While taking of the issue of *convention*, Austin holds that 'The illocutionary act is a conventional act; an act done as conforming to a convention.' For instance, in the cricket ground, when the umpire of the match says out!, then the term out! is sufficient for the performance of the act. Likewise, when a couple says before the registrar that *I do this woman my lawful wedded spouse*, then merely this utterance is ample proof for marriage. Plainly, there is a convention, in which merely utterance of certain word by certain person in certain circumstances is adequate for the successful performance of an act. Strawson, however, argued that there may be some plausible cases, where convention doesn't decide the force of an utterance. "It seems clear, that is, that there are many cases in which the illocutionary force of an utterance, though not exhausted by its meaning, is not owed to any *conventions* other than those which help to give it its meaning."[52] For example, 'Don't go'. This utterance may be a kind of request, or an order or as an entreaty and the like. There is no any convention which decides the locus of the force in this utterance. The thing which decides the force of this utterance is: "......the speaker's situation, hearer's attitude, manner, and the current intention."[53] Strawson, therefore, argued that if convention does not decide the force of an utterance, then why Austin unnecessarily generalized the theory that illocutionary act is a conventional act. As he wrote,

"It seems perfectly clear that, if at least we take the expressions convention and conventional in the most natural way, the doctrine of the conventional nature of the illocutionary act does not hold generally. Some illocutionary acts are conventional; others are not (except in so far as they are locutionary acts). Why then does Austin repeatedly affirm the contrary? It is unlikely that he has made the simple mistake of generalizing from some cases to all."[54]

Secondly, Strawson considered on *securing of uptake*. It means that the hearer or audience must understand the meaning along with the illocutionary force of an utterance. However, there are some perplexities involved in it. For example, a man presents a bequest, or gift to someone on the certain occasion. In such a situation, no one reads his desire or will or instructions, whatever he wrote on the gift. Thus, the *aim* but not the *achievement* is important for the illocutionary act. "We may be tempted to say instead that at least *the aim, if not the achievement*, of securing uptake is an essential element in the performance of the illocutionary act."[55] This contention is, however, problematic. Let me suppose that a man does not present a gift in real sense, but he merely feels satisfaction in his thought that I have presented the gift. In such a case, may I say that this kind of satisfaction which occurred in the thought will be conceived as an illocutionary act. While responding to this objection, Strawson wrote, "But this objection at most forces on us an amendment to which we are in any case obliged, namely, that the aim, if not the achievement, of securing uptake is essentially a *standard, if not an invariable*, element in the performance of the illocutionary act. So the analysis of the aim of securing uptake remains an essential element in the analysis of the notion of the illocutionary act."[56]

Strawson further argued that for the successful illocutionary act, it is indispensable that the hearer not only understands and but also recognizes the intention of the speaker. However, there are many cases, when the recognition by the audience is not necessary. In these cases, the speaker merely utters something without considering whether the hearer or the addressee recognizes his judgment or not. For instance, in the law court, when the judge gives his/her verdict, naturally he doesn't consider whether the petitioner recognizes his/her verdict or not. Likewise, in a cricket ground, when the umpire says out! then he doesn't think that the audience recognizes his judgment. In these cases, the role of convention must increase. As Strawson wrote, "But as we move further into the region of institutionalized procedures, the strain becomes too much for the scheme to bear. On the one, one of its basic features—namely, the reference to an intention to secure a definite response in an audience (over and above the securing of uptake)—has to be dropped. On the other, the reference to social conventions of procedures assumes a very much greater importance."[57]

Strawson, therefore, endeavours to show that there is not only one criterion which decides the functioning of the language. It varies due to variation of contexts. It may be delineated in the following ways:

- Firstly, language works in accordance with convention governed practices. For instance, when umpire says out! or the judges pass their judgment and so forth, then merely these utterances are adequate for the performance of an act.
- Secondly, in the some other cases, language works regarding the intention of the speaker as well as its recognition by the hearer. For instance, when the speaker says to the hearer that 'don't go'. Its meaning doesn't ascertain by convention. It is decided by the interpersonal relationship between the speaker and the hearer. In such a situation the hearer's recognition is indispensable.
- Thirdly, there are some other cases, when the intention of the speaker is important but its recognition by the hearer is trivial. For instance, let me suppose that a person is working in a company, whose job is publicity of the company products. Naturally, he will give a lot of information about his company products to the addressee without considering their recognitions. The recognition of the speaker's intention by the hearer is, therefore, not important in all cases.

While elucidating this, Strawson said, "I have set in sharp contrast those cases in which the overt intention is simply to forward a definite and convention-governed practice (for example, a game) in a definite way provided for by the conventions or rules of the practice and those cases in which the overt intention includes that of securing a definite response (cognitive or practical) in an audience over and above that which is necessarily secured if uptake is secured. But there is something misleading about the sharpness of this contrast; and it would certainly be wrong to suppose that all cases fall clearly and neatly into one or another of these two classes. A speaker whose job it is to do so may offer information, instructions, or even advice, and yet be overtly indifferent as to whether or not his information is accepted as such, his instructions followed, or his advice taken. His wholly overt intention may amount to no more than that of making available—in a 'take it or leave it' spirit—to his audience the information or instructions or opinion in question....."[58]

L.J. Cohen, in his article, *Do Illocutionary Forces Exist?* criticised Austin's speech act theory. Earlier, we have mentioned that Austin distinguished between the *meaning* and the *force* in the light of the locutionary act and the illocutionary act. Cohen, however, advocated that the distinction between force and meaning hinges upon false presumption to the extent that force is not entirely separate from its meaning. If Austin were to understand the real sense of meaning, he would have never distinguished between force and meaning. He further said that if one subtly observes Austin's contention, he/she may say that even Austin himself conceived that the force underlies in its meaning. Cohen considers a couple of Austin's examples, when Austin assumes that except exclamations like 'damn!' or 'ouch!' each utterance is both the locutionary as well as the illocutionary act. As Austin wrote, "....... whenever I 'say' something (except perhaps a mere exclamation like 'damn' and 'ouch'). I shall be performing both locutionary and illocutionary act."[59] Further, "....... The locutionary act as much as the illocutionary is an abstraction only: every genuine speech act is both."[60] Moreover, "When we have an explicit performative we also have an illocutionary act."[61] For example, when we say, "I warn you that........' or 'I order you to.........' as an explicit performative, we also perform the act of warning and ordering, respectively. If these utterances are both locutionary as well as illocutionary act, and then how can I distinguish the force from its meaning? Cohen, therefore, advocated that it will be untenable to say that the force is separate from its meaning. As Cohen wrote, "In short, what Austin calls the illocutionary force of an utterance is that aspect of its meaning which is either conveyed by its explicitly performative prefix, if it has one, or might have been so conveyed by the use of such an expression. Any attempt to prise off this aspect of meaning, and regard it not as meaning but as something else, leads to paradox and confusion."[62]

In this regards, Cohen makes some valuable observations which plainly show that the force is contained in its meaning. Firstly, Cohen conceived that the meaning of the utterance varies due to variations of the utterance's *intonation*. When a person says something in the falling tones, its meaning may be different, from the same thing which is said in raising tones. For instance, 'It is raining'. When a person says it simply, then it is clearly a descriptive statement. But when a person says it with raising tone, this utterance will be treated as warning. Indeed, the role of intonation is very important in deciding the meaning of an utterance. We, therefore, can't separate the force from the meaning. Cohen remarked, "The difference between a rising and a falling intonation has as much of a right to affect the classification of individual utterances into English sentences as has the difference of sound between raining and hailing. There are pitch phonemes as well as vowel and consonant ones so that attention to the meaning of the sentence-type cannot justify a distinction between the meaning and the illocutionary force of such utterances."[63]

Secondly, Cohen attempted to show that the meaning of an utterance not only underpins over its intonation but also on the circumstances in which the utterance is used. For example, 'Go to Patna tomorrow!' may be treated as a command or as an order or a request or a recommendation or a piece of advice. It is totally hinged upon the circumstances and more so the intention of the speaker. Likewise, 'He lost his case.' When a traveller will say this utterance at the railway platform, its meaning will be entirely different, when this utterance will be said by a client in the antechamber of a law-court. It reveals that the same utterance can be used on varied contexts for varied purposes and according to purposes and contexts, it acquires diverse meanings. Thus, the force is not separable from its meaning. While emphasizing this Cohen wrote, "Here again it seems as though the individual utterance has not only a meaning, derived immediately from the general meaning of the sentence-type—the highest common factor, as it were, of all the sentence-type's possible uses—but also an illocutionary force, dependent upon its own, rather more special, circumstances."[64]

Thirdly, Cohen asserted that the meaning of the utterance can be of a general kind in which an utterance has generally been used and also can be of a particular kind in which the utterance has been used in the specific conditions, like in the law-court. For example, 'I wish you good afternoon'; this utterance has been by and large used for wishes. Instead, it might be used as denial of the audience, which is the opposite of wishes. On this ground, Cohen suggested that the force of the utterance is not completely separate from its meaning. "....... The utterance has the sentence-pattern's common role as a basic meaning, and the dismissal as an additional feature, its illocutionary force, dependent partly on this basis meaning and partly on contextual circumstances."[65]

Fourthly, Cohen emphasised that in all likelihood, the speaker utters something and the hearer could not understand the speaker's intention. The speaker, therefore, does not succeed in producing effect, which he would like to communicate to the hearer or addressee. For example, 'Go to Patna tomorrow!' It may be possible that the speaker utters this statement as request, while the hearer takes it as an order. Likewise, 'He hit her'. In this utterance, it is very difficult to find out whether *he* refers to her husband or her lover or her brother or her father. It reveals that force is not separate from its meaning. As he asserted, "It then seems plausible to suggest that the force of the original utterance is distinguishable from its meaning, on the ground that what was understood at once was the meaning and what was in doubt until it had been clarified was the force. But it would in general be better practice to say explicitly how much of the intended meaning was understood at once and how much was not."[66]

Cohen further distinguished between *what is said* and the act of saying it. For example, an army officer says to a journalist, "The fighter MIG 37 is useless." Although, this statement is verifiable, depending to the fact that the fighter MIG 37 is useless or not. In this respect, this utterance may be true or false. However, an important question is: Is it useful for security purpose to leak such secret matter? Obviously, the leakage of such confidential report will not be advantageous. In such a situation, the journalist found himself in the state of topsy-turvy. Hence, the journalist may be confused about *what the army officer said* or about his act of saying. According to Cohen, where the former requires clarification of meaning, the latter requires something else like force. In the word of Cohen, "If what the civil servant said may be true or false in virtue of its meaning, the act of saying it must surely have something else, its force, in virtue of which it can be justified or unjustified, valid or invalid, happy or unhappy."[67]

By virtue of the above contention, Cohen endeavours to show that the distinction between locutionary and illocutionary act is untenable. It is alright that the meaning is related with locutionary act while the force is concerned with illocutionary act. However, if the distinction between locutionary and illocutionary act is not justifiable, how could the distinction between the meaning and the force be sustained? Furthermore, when Austin considered the performative utterances, he plainly distinguished between two sorts of utterances; explicit and implicit utterances. For example, 'I promise to go there' and 'I shall go there', both utterances are performative. However, the difference in the both utterances is that the former is *explicit* while the later is *implicit*. While emphasizing this, Cohen argued, "If all utterances turn out to be performative, then instead of distinguishing some utterances from others it looks as though we have to distinguish one aspect of every utterance from another. We have to regard all utterances as dual, as it were..... But all this philosophical inflation, and consequential coining of new technical terms, can be avoided if we keep 'performative' as a term applicable to verbs, verb-uses, particles, adverbs, phrases or meanings rather than to sentences or whole utterances. We can then make all the further distinctions we need between, say, what is explicitly performative at all (*e.g.*, 'I promise'), semi-explicitly performative (*e.g.* 'without fail'), inexplicitly performative (*e.g.* 'I shall') or not performative at all (*e.g.*, 'that I shall go'). There is no need now for the locutionary-illocutionary distinction."[68] Cohen, therefore, brushed aside the distinction between the force and the meaning and advocated that force is not entirely separate from the meaning. In other words, if we conceive meaning in the wide sense, it must contain force also. The concept of *illocutionary force* of the utterance which is suggested by Austin is, therefore, untenable.

Mat Furberg, in his article, *Meaning and Illocutionary Force*, reinterpreted Austin's theory about illocutionary force and criticised Cohen's contention. Earlier, we have seen that Cohen argued that the force is contained in its meaning. As he wrote, "I shall sketch an unorthodox reinterpretation of Austin's doctrine of illocutionary force and try to show that it withstands Cohen's type of criticism."[69]

Firstly, Furberg suggested that the term *act* is misleading. This term should not be used in the sense of locutionary or illocutionary act. It is only applicable in the case of action. In this sense, statement and promising can't be *acts* while the *act of stating* and *the act of promising* are necessarily be acts. A statement can be true or false but what has made it true or false? Merely the *act of stating*, but not the statement in itself. Likewise, *promising* can be true or false due to the act of promising. It reveals that this term is not applicable in terms of speech acts but it is only applicable in the result of such acts. Austin, however, ignored this study and generalized the term *act* for all sorts of acts. For this very reason, Furberg didn't use the term act. Instead, he preferred the use of the term *dimension* or *episode* on the place of *act*. While emphasizing this, he said, "Austin often speaks as if inquiries into the locutionary and the illocutionary dimension of an utterance are inquiries into different aspects of a speech *episode*. But this practice betrays that he is not really much concerned about speech acts at all; he is concerned about dimensions of results of such acts or episodes.....I suggest that the statement or the promise is a result of an act of stating or promising, and that Austin's inquiries into the locutionary and the illocutionary dimensions are inquiries such a semantic result. But then the study of locutionary and the illocutionary dimension is not a study of any act at all..... This terminology of 'act'. is very misleading."[70]

Well, Furberg's contention is that the term *act* is not appropriate in the sense of *act*; it should be used in the sense of *action* rather than speech. Hence, the term *promise* is not an *act* but the *act of promising* is necessarily an act. However, when we subtly examine this contention, we may say that this distinction is mistaken. We may ask: Is promise different from the act of promising? Indeed, there are some utterances of whose pronunciation is adequate *per se* for action, like promise, warning, advising, and so forth. Thus, there is no difference between promise and the act of promise. When a person utters 'I promise', it means that he does promise. In this sense saying is equivalent to doing. When Austin used this term, he was aware of this fact so he maintained that *every speech is an act, e.g.*, an utterance does not only state something but also it performs some action in real sense. Thus, there is no ambiguity in this term.

When Austin says that the meaning and the force of the utterance are deduced by convention. Furberg alleges that Austin has shrugged off the importance of the current speaker and also the current hearer. When we ascertain the meaning of an utterance, we must consider on the role of current speaker and hearer's intention. As he writes, "And Austin's stress on the conventionality of the illocutionary dimension minimizes the importance of the current addressee as well as of the current speaker. Illocutionary force becomes next of kin to meaning. In an established language, it would be disastrous to define these relatives in terms of the current speaker's intentions and/or the current audience's uptake of these intentions."[71] This contention is important in the sense that when we ascertain the meaning of an utterance, we should emphasize on the intention of the current speaker and the current hearer. Albeit, Austin takes into account on the intention of the speaker but he doesn't recognized on the perspective of the hearer. If we shrugged off the role of the hearer, there may be a communication gap between the speaker and the hearer.

Furberg, furthermore, argued that Austin, at the end of his book *How to Do Things with Words*, attempted to submerge the performative utterance and illocutionary act. This contention is preposterous. According to him, there are some fundamental differences between the performatives and illocutionary force. The illocutionary force is plainly related with language, while the performative utterance is bound up with the action. As Furberg wrote, "Illocutionary force is integral to my utterance as linguistic utterance; performativeness has no necessary connection with language at all."[72] He further assumed that the acceptance of the first person, singular, present, indicative active as proposed by Austin for his classic explicit performative would lead to several conceptual problems. Furberg pointed out numerous examples of classic explicit performative which failed to fulfil this touchstone. He, however, cited some examples, which are really fulfilled the touchstones of classic explicit performatives and called it *archetypal performatives*. "But there remain utterances which meet Austin's general demands on classic explicit performatives. Among them are the ceremonial formulae employed in the institutional procedures of acquitting, convicting, appointing, demoting, excommunicating, baptizing, and naming. I call them *archetypal performatives*."[73]

Furberg, moreover, distinguished between the explicit illocutionary force and archetypal performatives. Firstly, the explicit illocutionary acts are in a certain sense ancillary inasmuch as they demand supplementation. The examples of explicit illocutionary acts may be, 'I promise you so and so,' or 'I warn you' or 'I advise you' and the like. Indeed, these examples demand a content for their successful performance, otherwise nothing will be 'promised' or 'warned' or 'advised'. While, archetypal performatives is self-sufficient. For instance,

'I can acquit you'. Plainly, this example is self-verifying and there is no need for any other content.

In addition to this, Furberg accepted that the classic illocutionary acts may be of two other kinds—the theoretical and the practical. For example, 'I forecast that we shall go tomorrow' is theoretical. Whereas, 'I promise that I shall go tomorrow' is practical. According to Furberg, both sorts of utterances involve a kind of obligation but these are different in the degrees of commitment. The former example doesn't indicate certainty, Furberg called it the *prognostic formula,* while the later is underpinned upon certainty which he called the *promisory formula.* As he wrote, "......the shouldering of certain obligations, different to different discourses and degrees of commitment. A person who, in the right circumstances, has used a prognostic formula seems to have created a forecast in about the same way as a man who, in the right circumstances, has used a promissory formula has made a promise."[74] Furberg further contended that there are basically two differences between both of them. "First, in using a promisory illocutionary formula I have not merely made a promise but I am also committing myself so to act that the world will conform to my words. Secondly, in promising I have not merely bound myself to the topic (as in forecasting) but also made a personal commitment to the addressee."[75]

Furberg moreover distinguished between the illocutionary act and archetypal performatives in terms of the obligation of future. The illocutionary acts in some senses, involve the obligation of future, whereas, archetypal performatives do not involve the obligation of future. Secondly, the later is fundamentally addressee-directed, while the former is in spite of its grammatical appearance, directed to society at large. Thirdly, the archetypal performatives may be non-verbal. While, the explicit illocutionary act cannot be non-verbal. As he wrote, "Although there are non-verbal equivalents of the illocutionary phrases, there is no non-verbal equivalents of the whole speech act: there must always be an essentially linguistic supplementation, to the correct uptake of which the verbal or non-verbal illocutionary devices are ancillaries."[76]

In addition to this, Furberg criticised Cohen's arguments that the force of utterances has comprised in its meaning. While, Furberg claimed, "I do not contend that in Austin's writings there is a hard line to be drawn between meaning and illocutionary force, between the locutionary and the illocutionary dimension of an utterance. But I do contend the arguments now scrutinized have not shown that there is nothing to Austin's doctrine of illocutionary force—though it remains vague and intuitive, and in pressing need of more elucidation. And above all I contend that in the discussion of Cohen's objections there have emerged reasons for holding that there are two distinguishable aspects of what an utterance conveys in a rule-governed and well-established manner."[77] While commenting upon this Cohen wrote, "Nor did I claim that 'there is nothing to Austin's doctrine of illocutionary force', only that the concept of illocutionary force, as Austin himself defines it, is empty."[78]

In this context, it will be important to consider the contribution of G.J. Warnock. Warnock in his book *J.L. Austin,* raised many questions about Austin's doctrine. One of the most important question is related to the *force* and the *meaning* of the utterances. Cohen emphasised that the force of the utterance has contained in its meaning. Furberg brushed aside Cohen's argument and mentioned that there are some differences between the force and the meaning. It seems that Warnock adopted the mid-way between Cohen and Furberg. Warnock, on the other hand, conceived that by and large illocutionary act is determined by locutionary act. In such a situation, meaning and force became inseparable to each other. ".......illocutionary act is fully determined, as it were, by his locutionary act—the force of the utterance is, in this case not 'detachable' from its meaning....."[79] He, on the other hand, contended that if the divergent will emerge between what is meant and how it was to be taken, then the force is detachable from its meaning. While emphasizing this Warnock argued, "He wished to 'distinguish force and meaning' on the basis that these are often, even standardly, separable and different: to establish 'what was meant' by what a speaker said is usually not to establish what he meant it as, how it was to be 'taken';...... To say that the force and the meaning are in general different is not to deny that—sometimes—the one may include the other."[80]

Searle, in his earlier contributions, also distinguished between the meaning and the force in the light of the distinction between *'have meaning'* and *'mean something'*.[81] Searle conceded that 'Have meaning' is concerned with literal meaning while 'mean something' is related to the *force* of the utterance. While highlighting this distinction, Searle emphasises two sorts of devices: the *proposition-indicating device* and the *function-indicating device*. Proposition-indicating device reveals the literal meaning, whereas function-indicating device is bound up with the *force* of the utterance. "........the sentence has two parts, the proposition-indicating element and the function-indicating device. The function-indicating device shows how the proposition is to be taken, or, to put it in another way, what illocutionary force the utterance is to have, that is, what illocutionary act the speaker is performing in the utterance of the sentence. Function-indicating devices in English include word order, stress, intonation contour, punctuation, the mood of the verb, and finally, a set of so-called performative verb."[82] Apart from this, in his recent formulation, *'How Performatives Work'*(1989) Searle writes, "In *Speech Acts* (1969) and other writings I pointed out that in general, illocutionary acts have the structure F(*p*), where the "F" stands for the illocutionary force, and the "(p)" stands for the propositional content. If communication is to be successful, the hearer has to be able to figure out from the hearing the sentence what is the illocutionary force and what is the propositional content. In the sentence, 'It is raining,' the propositional content expressed is: that it is raining, and the illocutionary force of a statement is indicated by such things as word order, intonation contour, mood of the verb and punctuation."[83] Later, Searle himself conceives as to this typology is *"right* but *incomplete"*.[84] He, therefore, rejects this distinction and calls it *declaration*. "In the *Foundation of Illocutionary Logic*, (Searle and Vanderveken, 1985) Daniel Vanderveken and I argued that performative utterances were all case of declarations......In a declaration of the form F(p) the successful performance of the speech act is to change the world to make it the case that p. Declarations thus have simultaneously both the word-to-world and the world-to-word directions of fit."[85]

Apparently, the problem of the force and the meaning is debatable issue among philosophers. On the one hand, a group of philosophers believe that there is no force *inter alia* the meaning. A group of some other philosophers, on the other hand, contend that meaning and force are detachable from each other. A word or sentence is used in different context and according to context, it acquires varied meaning. Thus, there is no certainty of meaning. However, when we ponder over this issue at the subtle and deeper levels, we may say that there is a clear-cut difference between force and meaning especially in Austin's philosophy. Although Austin advocates that 'the locutionary act as much as the illocutionary is an abstraction only: every genuine speech act is both'. It doesn't mean there is no difference between the meaning and the force. He himself conceived that the only way to distinguish between the locutionary and the illocutionary act is meaning and force. The locutionary act is bound up with *meaning* while the illocutionary act is concerned with the *force*; 'I want to distinguish force and meaning in the sense in which meaning is equivalent to sense and reference.....'

We may say then that the meaning of an utterance underpins over numerous factors, for instance; literal meaning, speaker's intention, hearer's personality, interpersonal relationship between the speaker and the hearer, context, intonation and so forth. If it is correct, then we will be bound to accept the distinction between the meaning and the force. This study leads us to think that if we don't accept the difference of meaning and force, we will be unable to understand all facets of meanings of an utterance, and thereby there must arise a communication gap between the speaker and the hearer. In such a situation, the speaker will say something and the hearer will understand something else. Thus, it can be said that meaning and force are distinct to each other.

## REFERENCES


1. Austin, J.L. (1982): *How to Do Things with Words*, edited by J.O. Urmson and Marina Sbisa, p. 148.
2. Cerf, Walter (1969): *Critical review of How to Do Things with Words.* In K.T. Funn (Ed.), Symposium on J.L. Austin, p. 356.
3. Austin, J.L. (1982): *How to Do Things with Words*, edited by J.O. Urmson and Marina Sbisa, p. 95.
4. *Ibid.* p. 96.
5. *Ibid.* p. 96.
6. Austin, J.L. (1979): *Truth.* In J.O. Urmson and G.J. Warnock (Eds), Philosophical papers, pp. 121-22.
7. Warnock, G.J. (1989): *J.L. Austin*, p. 121.
8. *Ibid.* p. 121.
9. Austin, J.L. (1982): *How to Do Things with Words*, edited by J.O. Urmson and Marina Sbisa, p. 98.
10. *Ibid.* p. 95.
11. *Ibid.* p. 94.
12. Cerf, Walter (1969): *Critical review of How to Do Things with Words.* In K.T. Funn (Ed.), Symposium on J.L. Austin, pp. 356-57.
13. Austin, J.L. (1982): *How to Do Things with Words*, edited by J.O. Urmson and Marina Sbisa, p. 146.
14. Cerf, Walter (1969): *Critical review of How to Do Things with Words.* In K.T. Funn (Ed.), Symposium on J.L. Austin, p. 357.
15. Warnock, G.J. (1989): J.L. Austin, p. 149.
16. Austin, J.L. (1982): *How to Do Things with Words*, edited by J.O. Urmson and Marina Sbisa, pp. 98-99.
17. *Ibid.* p. 98.
18. *Ibid.* p. 95.
19. Cerf, Walter (1969): *Critical review of How to Do Things with Words.* In K.T. Funn (Ed.), Symposium on J.L. Austin, p. 357.
20. Strawson, P.F. (1964): *Intention and Convention in Speech Acts*, The Philosophical Review, Vol. LXXIII, No. 4. Edited in J.R. Searle (1979): The Philosophy of Language, p. 38.
21. Austin, J.L. (1982): *How to Do Things with Words*, edited by J.O. Urmson and Marina Sbisa, p. 101.
22. Warnock, G.J. (1989): *J.L. Austin*, p. 130.
23. Furberg, M. (1969): *Locutionary and Illocutionary Acts.* In K.T. Funn (Ed), Symposium on J.L. Austin, p. 449.
24. Austin, J.L. (1982): *How to Do Things with Words*, edited by J.O. Urmson and Marina Sbisa, p. 105.
25. Warnock, G.J. (1989): *J.L. Austin*, pp. 123-24.
26. Graham, Keith. (1977): *J.L. Austin: Critique of Ordinary Language Philosophy*, p. 91.

27. Austin, J.L. (1982): *How to Do Things with Words*, edited by J.O. Urmson and Marina Sbisa, p. 103.
28. *Ibid.* p. 121.
29. *Ibid.* p. 119.
30. *Ibid.* p. 109.
31. *Ibid.* pp. 121-22.
32. Warnock, G.J. (1989): *J.L. Austin*, p. 130.
33. Furberg, M. (1969): *Locutionary and Illocutionary Acts.* In K.T.Funn (Ed), Symposium on J.L. Austin, p. 446.
34. Alston, W. p. (1982): *Philosophy of Language*, p. 36.
35. Austin, J.L. (1982): *How to Do Things with Words*, edited by J.O. Urmson and Marina Sbisa, pp. 116-18.
36. *Ibid.* p. 103.
37. Ibid pp. 116-117.
38. Austin, J.L. (1975): *How to Do Things with Words.* In J.O. Urmson and Marina Sbisa (Eds.), p. 134.
39. *Ibid.* p. 140.
40. *Ibid.* p. 141.
41. Warnock, G.J. (1989): *J.L. Austin*, p. 135.
42. Austin, J.L. (1975): *How to do Things with Words.* In J.O. Urmson and Marina Sbisa (Eds.), p. 144.
43. *Ibid.* p. 143.
44. *Ibid.* p. 145.
45. *Ibid.* p. 148.
46. *Ibid.* p. 151.
47. *Ibid.* pp. 151-52.
48. *Ibid.* p. 146.
49. Cerf, W. (1969): *Critical review of How to Do Things with Words.* In K.T. Fann (Ed.), Symposium on J.L. Austin, pp. 359-60.
50. *Ibid.* p. 369.
51. *Ibid.* p. 371.
52. Strawson, P. F. (1969): *Intention and Convention in Speech Acts.* In K.T. Fann (Ed.), Symposium on J.L. Austin, p. 384.
53. *Ibid.* p. 385.
54. *Ibid.* p. 385.
55. *Ibid.* p. 389.
56. *Ibid.* p. 389.
57. *Ibid.* pp. 395-96.
58. *Ibid.* pp. 399-400.
59. Austin, J.L. (1975): *How to Do Things with Words.* In J.O. Urmson and Marina Sbisa (Eds.), p. 133.
60. *Ibid.* p. 147.
61. *Ibid.* p. 132.
62. Cohen, L.J. (1969): *Do Illocutionary Forces Exist?* In K.T. Fann (Ed.), Symposium on J.L. Austin, p. 429.

63. *Ibid.* p. 430.
64. *Ibid.* pp. 430-431.
65. *Ibid.* p. 431.
66. *Ibid.* p. 432.
67. *Ibid.* p. 435.
68. *Ibid.* p. 439.
69. Furberg, M. (1969): *Meaning and Illocutionary Force.* In K.T. Fann (Ed.), Symposium on J.L. Austin, p. 445.
70. *Ibid.* pp. 446-47.
71. *Ibid.* p. 448.
72. *Ibid.* p. 452.
73. *Ibid.* p. 452.
74. *Ibid.* p. 453.
75. *Ibid.* pp. 454-55.
76. *Ibid.* p. 467.
77. *Ibid.* p. 467.
78. *Ibid.* p. 468.
79. Warnock, G.J. (1989): *J.L. Austin*, p. 149.
80. *Ibid.* pp. 149-50.
81. Searle, J. R. (1979): *'The Philosophy of Language'*(Ed), p. 44.
82. *Ibid.* pp. 43-44.
83. Searle, J.R. (1989): *'How Performatives Work'*, Linguistics and Philosophy, p. 540.
84. *Ibid.* p. 540.
85. *Ibid.* p. 541.

# 6

# Non-Verbal Speech Act

The distinction of the constative and the performative utterance is fused in the speech act theory. As we have seen Austin classified speech act into the locutionary, the illocutionary, and the perlocutionary act. The locutionary act is an act *of saying* something; the illocutionary act is an act of *in saying* something; and the perlocutionary act is an act of *by saying* something. Eventually, Austin emphasised on the illocutionary act and thereby the locutionary and the perlocutionary act gradually faded.

The question is: why Austin emphasised on the illocutionary act? Why did he not emphasize on the locutionary and the perlocutionary acts? So far as I understand, the locutionary act is concerned with saying something in the full normal sense, while the perlocutionary act is concerned with its consequence, *i.e.*, what effect we impose upon the hearer. Both of the things are trivial from the speaker's point of view. When a speaker uses an utterance, *in saying* something, he/she endeavours to successfully communicate his/her thought and intention to the listener. By virtue of this, he/she produces some *force* in his/her utterance. Actually, the speaker's job is neither to get certain result nor merely to say something redundantly. He simply wants that the hearer successfully understands his intention or motive, whatever he would like to communicate. On this account, Austin emphasised on *securing of uptake* for the illocutionary act.

It may be argued that if the speaker would like to communicate his intention to the hearer or addressee, it is *sine qua non* as to the hearer must understand the intention of the speaker (*e.g.*, the meaning and the force). If he does not deem the speaker's intention, the act would not be illocutionary act. In other words, in such a situation the speaker intends to produce a certain illocutionary effects in the hearer and he intends to produce the effect by getting the hearer to recognize his intention. Thus, two things are important for the illocutionary act:

- Firstly, the securing of uptakes.
- Secondly, it should be recognized by the hearer.

There are many direct or indirect ways by which the hearer intends to produce a certain illocutionary effects in the hearer. When the speaker uses some utterances and the hearer directly uptakes the intention of the speaker, the act would be *direct speech act*. A few examples of the direct speech act are as follows: I give and bequeath my house to my brother; I order you don't go ahead; I warn you that there is a vicious bull in the field; I inaugurate this seminar, and so forth.

There are some other cases when the speaker does not say something directly, *viz.*, sometimes, his utterance directly sounds like a statement; however, indirectly it produces certain force on the hearer. In such circumstances, the speaker communicates his ideas to the hearer indirectly and the hearer indubitably uptakes the speaker's intention. For instance, suppose someone is taking food on the dining table and in the meantime, a person utters; *'can you pass the salt'*? Here, he is plainly requesting to pass the salt and the other person clearly understands his intention without any ambiguity. Likewise, a person comes from outside and sits in a chamber and then he utters, *'I feel suffocation in this room'*. It simply implies that please open the windows and doors of this room. By and large, there is no controversy between the speaker and the hearer. Such sorts of utterances are known as *indirect speech act*. J.R. Searle developed and modified the *indirect speech act* in his varied formulations. In his book, *Expression and Meaning* (1979), he argued, "In indirect speech acts the speaker communicates to the hearer more than he actually says by way of relying on their mutually shared background information, both linguistic and non-linguistic, together with the general powers of rationality and inference on the part of the hearer."[1] Moreover, he claimed that the avoidance of indirect speech act creates more problems in ethics. As he wrote, "Many confusions in recent moral philosophy rest on a failure to understand the nature of such indirect speech acts".[2]

The above discussion, delineates the fact that the seminal point of the illocutionary act is securing of uptake along with its recognition by the hearer for the successful communication. *If it is true, then it can be done in some other ways, like non-verbally. In other words, we may say that the intention of indicating, requesting, warning, and the like, can be systematically expressed non-verbally. If we shrug off the role of non-verbal speech act in our life then not only our practical life but also our entire spiritual life would be greatly affected. In every walk of life, non-verbal expressions are displayed, received and influenced by us.* For example, if a person is solely smiling and not saying anything at all, still one can precisely infer the intention of the smiling person. No direct and indirect speech act can explain such sort of silent acts. Furthermore, in the cricket ground, when a player is out, the umpire does not say anything. He just raises his finger and his decision gets communicated to all and the observers either get in applause and clapping or feel sad by lowering their heads. All these acts in this episode facilitate the powerful impact of the non-verbal speech act. Likewise, in the domain of spirituality, the highest expressions are silence or not this—not this.

The non-verbal act may have three important dimensions: *visible, invisible* and *paralinguistic*. Visible dimension is the most important facet of non-verbal speech act. By and large, it may be expressed by gesture or body language, eye contact and facial expressions and the like.

*Body language* is the powerful source of expression of our ideas or intentions. For instance, when a teacher is delivering a lecture in the classroom, some students who are not interested in the lecture may express their intention by body movements. Similarly, when you see off your friends or relatives, you hold up your hand, open palm and turning up like pendulum. It simply reveals to bye-bye or good-by. Many body movements generally convey specific information or directions like, stop, go, come, sit down, yes, no, good-by and so on. These expressions are not less powerful than the verbal expressions.

*Eye contact* is an interesting device to communicate our ideas and intentions. We can plainly observe the application of eye contact in our practical life, like body language. For instance, if a person maintains his eye contact with another person for a long time, it simply refers the demonstration of attraction. On the other hand, breaking of eye contact is usually a sign of avoidance. Likewise, prolonged eye contact may be indication of threat. For instance, when the teacher is delivering lecture, and if some students gossip, the teacher may merely locate these students and look at them. Subsequently, the student becomes silent. Eye contact may be used to seek attention of others.

*Facial expression* is also a specific medium of expression of our ideas. When a person is in trouble or pleasure, he expresses his sorrow or happiness by facial expression. Plainly, when a person, is suffering from pain, he may show expressions on his face. In this situation, we can clearly judge his position. Likewise, when a student gets first class in his M.A. examination, he expresses his happiness by a smiling face. Facial expression is an interesting way of mimicry. Similarly, it can be an appropriate medium of expression about sympathy and empathy.

Moreover, deaf and dumb persons always express their thought, intention, motive, emotions, etc., using creativity visible expressions and gestures which are known as *sign language. These forms of expressions are medium of communication without use of verbal language*. We, therefore, can't gainsay the importance of the body language, eye contact and facial expressions in communication.

*Invisible dimension* may be an important source of communication by which we gracefully express our motives, intentions and propensities to the hearer. Sometimes, a person expresses his thoughts or intentions neither by using any visible dimensions nor by use of language. He just maintains silence of and endeavours to be expressionless. This sort of silence, however, communicates something. The observer may attribute some meaning to the state of silence the person being observed. Attribution of meaning, however, will be determined by the intention and contextual factors. For instance, complete silence in a tragic situation insinuates profound grief. However, such silence in interpersonal interaction may mean lack of interest or indifference. Thus, in this sense, silence may be a sort of language without words. For example, you are asking somebody for something, but he does not respond at all. Through his silence, he expresses his view clearly, and the observer (in such circumstances) makes judgment about such silence. Silence is one of best method to express annoyance or irritation. Suppose you are the head of the institution and someone of your organisation is not performing his duty appropriately. In this situation, you may express your irritation by silence or by ignoring him. Here, silence would be much more effective *vis-à-vis* any other sort of verbal language or non-verbal expression.

Generally, one incorrectly understands that this procedure has always been used in the negative sense while it has been used in the both senses negative as well as affirmative. For instance, when a person asks his friend: Would you like to go to cinema? The friend does not respond. He may take this silence as a positive or as a negative answer, contingent upon his understanding of intention inherent in silence of his friend including backgrounds and circumstances of the episode.

Another example, we may refer to the way Lord Buddha used to respond. When Lord Buddha was asked by anybody: Is the external world eternal or not or both or both not? Whether body and soul are identical or not? Does God exists or not? and so forth. Lord Buddha did not respond. His silence, however, was taken in both senses: negative as well as positive.

Moreover, all those philosophers, who believe in transcendental being, like God and soul, express by silence. They contend as to such sort of realities merely could be realized but not described by any process of language. So, those people who don't realize these things, can't understand by language. Language, by nature, merely communicates the physical and limited things, whereas, the transcendental being is metaphysical and unlimited. They, therefore, attempt to be expressionless or silent. It does not mean that such realities do not exist. They certainly exist, however, they are communicable by language to the extent that language merely communicates thoughts, while the unearthly beings are beyond our thoughts. Upaniṣads called them indescribable and not this—not this (*neti-neti*). The highest expression of such reality is silence.

In the Taittirīya Upaniṣad the doctrine of the five sheaths (Kośas) has been discussed like, Annamaya Kośa (Physical plane), Prāṇamaya Kośa (biological plane), Manomaya Kośa (Mental or Psychological plane), Vijñānamaya Kośa (Metaphysical plane) and Ānandamaya Kośa (Mystical plane). In the above Kośa, language may be useful untill Vijñānamaya Kośa. So, whenever we enter on the mystical plane (Ānandamaya Kośa) and above this plane, language becomes redundant. According to Ken Upaniṣad, "That which can't be spoken by the speech, but by which speech is made possible; that which can't be thought by the mind, but by which, they say, the mind thinks; that which can't be seen by the eye, but by which eye is made to see; that which can't be heard by the ear, but by which ear is made to hear; that which does not breath, but by which breath is made possible, know that alone to be the Brahman, not this which they worship outside."[3] Furthermore, "Those who have said as to I know Brahman, he actually does not know, but those who have said as to I do not know Brahman, he actually knows."[4] Obviously, the person who realises Brahman, becomes Brahman. (*Brahman Ved Brahmaiv Bhavati*).[5] In this stage of realisation, all sorts of dualism duly convert into non-dualism, then who will ask and who will hear.

The *paralinguistic medium* is used by a speaker to express or hide his intention. Although, a sentence has certain or definite meaning, notwithstanding on the basis of its force, the meaning varies with variations in pitch, intonation, cadence, rhythm, loudness, intention and so forth. Therefore, these are the most important factors for deciding the meaning of any sentence. In other words, we may say that the raising and the falling of the speech acquires different meaning. For instance, if a person simply says that it is raining, then it is like a descriptive statement which describes the actual situation. On the other hand, if he utters the same sentence in the raising tone, this statement is taken like a warning. Likewise, on the basis of its force or emphasis, even a sentence has varied meanings. Another example cited earlier explains further, *"Have you purchased this horse in ten thousand rupees?"* Superficially, this sentence sounds like a question, whose answer may be either yes or no. However, with variation of emphasis on different part or word of this utterance, its meanings do change. When emphasis is on *have you*, its meaning would be that you couldn't purchase this horse, inasmuch as this is beyond of your status or income. Here, the meaning of this utterance would be sarcastic. The speaker does not think that the horse is really purchased by the person who is being addressed. But when emphasis is on *this horse*, its meaning would be as to this horse is vicious or weak or not competent to serve the purpose of the buyer. Again, when emphasis is on *ten thousand*, its meaning would be that this amount is too much for this horse. Furthermore, when force is put on *purchase*, its meaning would be that you have not purchased this horse. It may even imply that you have stolen or hired this horse for sometimes and so forth. Indeed, the context of utterance, the intention of the speaker and variations in emphasis on certain words of utterances, appears to be the most important factor for determining the meaning of a sentence. Thus, the variation of pitch, intonation, and cadence of the utterance make manifold meanings of the utterance.

Another sort of paralinguistic dimension may be opposite or converse meaning, which is derived from intention rather than any other thing. For instance, a boy requests his mother for going to cinema. His mother smilingly says: you can't go. The boy, however, takes her statement as consent and goes to cinema. Likewise, a man puts up his proposal to a woman by saying 'I love you' and she accepts his proposal by responding 'I hate you'. Although, the actual meaning of 'I hate you' would be I don't like you nonetheless when she utters it with smiling face, its meaning becomes 'I like you'. Of course, if spoken language does not have a corresponding body language *i.e.*, saying 'no' with smile, the body language is trusted as the true indicator of intention and 'no' is interpreted as 'yes'. Thus, for the correct inference of intention, the body language is seen as more reliable device *vis-à-vis* spoken words.

A number of questions can be raised about non-verbal speech acts. One may argue as to non-verbal act is not a kind of language. Language means such expressions which contain certain sound with grammatically correct vocables, whereas, non-verbal expression doesn't fulfil these conditions. However, when we subtly observe this objection, we may say that this objection is not justifiable for language. Language is a vehicle to communicate our thought, intention, and idea, so that by any process, we communicate our thought or intention, may be called another sorts of language. It reveals that language is not only that expression which communicates verbally but also it is such an expression which is communicated non-verbally. On this account, an eminent Indian linguistic scholar Achārya Bhartṛhari, in his celebrated book "Vākyapadīya", conceded that there are three paces of Vāk[6] (*e.g.*, speech).

- Vaikharī Vāk
- Madhyamā Vāk
- Paśyantī Vāk

Vaikharī Vāk is the concrete form of sound, whatever we speak or hear by externally audible sense organs, like ear. It is audible and it has certain form and sequence. In Vaikharī Vāk, both the word and its meaning are completely differentiable from each other. Examples of Vaikharī Vāk are sound of an axle, of a cart, a drum, a flute, a vīna so on and so forth. The nature of second stage is inner, known as Madhyamā Vāk. This is purely a mental state, reflecting whatever we think by our mind and intellect. At that stage, the word and its meaning are also separable to each other nonetheless practically its distinction remains impossible. The hearer can't conceive the meaning of Madhyamā Vāk by external sense organs. Eventually, if we enter into innermost stage, the word and its meaning become indistinguishable to each other. This stage is beyond mind and intellect and known as Paśyantī Vāk. Only those people who have attained enlightenment can experience the meaning of Paśyantī Vāk. Furthermore, Bhartṣhari distinguished Paśyantī Vāk into two sorts[42]: lower and higher. Higher Paśyantī Vāk (*param-rupam*) is beyond all sorts of verbal usages. Apparently, this is the stage of non-dualism. Thus, Vaikharī Vāk is dualistic; Madhyamā Vāk is Viśiṣtādvaitic, whereas Paśyantī Vāk is non-dualistic.

While describing the above three stages of language or Vāk, K.A. Subramania Iyer writes, "As the Paśyanti is one; the word and the meaning are not yet differentiated in it. It is pre-mental stage. In the second, Madhyamā stage, the word and the meaning are differentiated from each other, but each one is still a unity. This is the mental stage because the text emphasizes its association with the *Buddhi.* The last stage Vaikharī is externalised stage. Its association is with *prāṇa* (breath) and *karaṇa* (Vocal organs). Here, both the word and the meaning are fully differentiated, not only from each other but also within each other is full differentiation. It is this which is known to the ordinary man and which is used in everyday life."[7]

Even Śaiva[8] system has accepted four stratums of speech (Vāk).

- Parā Vāk
- Paśyantī Vāk
- Madhyamā Vāk
- Vaikharī Vāk

The Parā Vāk is the stage of pure consciousness i.e., non-dualistic. At that stage, language and reality become identical to each other. Although, it is beyond space, time, name and form nonetheless it is the locus of all sorts of Vāk [Paśyantī, Madhyamā and Vaikharī]. Paśyantī is the first manifestation of Parā Vāk. At that stage, the word and the meaning are somehow differentiated, however, its distinction in real sense is very difficult. For instance, an idea may implicitly exist in our mind and may remain indistinguishable from it. However, presence of any immediate cause may make it explicit. Madhyamā is the second stage of the manifestation of Parā Vāk and also more concrete *vis-à-vis* the Paśyantī Vāk to the extent that the word and the meaning become more explicit. For instance, earlier to speech, we conceptualised an idea in our mind, then we express it in language. Thus, thought and speech are clearly distinguishable to each other. Eventually, Vaikharī Vāk is the externally concrete form of language, whatever, we speak and hear by external sense organs in our daily life.

The above four levels of languages may conceptualise by the following instance. An athlete firstly he thinks about race. This is the first stage like Parā Vāk. Here, everything is implicit. Secondly, when he enters the second stage, he mentally prepares for race. At that stage, he gains more clarity and certainty *inter alia* the first stage. The second stage may be called Paśyantī. In accordance with his thoughts, he reaches on the play ground, changes his dress and then gets ready for race. Here, it appears that he is about to race. However, he has not started his race. This stage is known as Madhyamā. Eventually, he starts his race. At this stage, everything becomes clear and overt. Thus, all sorts of possibilities mature into actualities. This is the fourth stage, which is known as Vaikharī Vāk. In spirituality, Vaikharī Vāk considered as the lowest sort of expression, which affect is the least *inter alia* the Parā, Paśyantī and Madhyamā.

In his celebrated book, *'Abhinavagupta: An Historical and Philosophical Study'*, K.C. Pandey holds, "The distinction of each one of the four forms of speech from the rest of them will become clear if we were to compare them with the four conditions of a seed which sends out its sprout. The Parā is like that condition of seed in which all the future forms of the sprout, according to Sākhya conception, exist in the state of absolute unity. The Paśyantī is just like that condition in which there is just the rise of that state which is responsible for the first perceptible development. It is just like self-preparation on the part of a person before he makes any perceptible movement to stir or jump. The third, i.e. Madhyamā is like the enlargement of seed in which though there is a perceptible change from the original condition yet the two (seed and sprout) can't be pointed out as distinct from each other in point of substratum. The last *i.e.*, Vaikharī is comparable to that condition in which the sprout has appeared as distinct from the seed and both are directly perceptible as distinct from each other in all respects not including that of the substratum."[9] Of course, invisible dimension is also powerful medium of expression of our ideas, intention, propensity and the like.

One may also argue that non-verbal speech act can't be universal procedure to communicate our ideas, intentions, motives etc. It must be contextual. If the speaker and the hearer are not familiar with the context, they can't communicate their ideas, intentions and so forth. However, this problem can also be applied for direct and indirect speech acts to the extent that the direct and indirect speech acts are also contextual. With the variation of the contexts, both the verbal and the non-verbal speech acts have different meanings.

Strictly speaking, sometimes, verbal speech acts become more obscure, equivocal and complex rather than non-verbal speech act. At that juncture, even context does not clarify its actual meaning. In such a situation, non-verbal speech act may be more helpful to facilitate understanding of the actual intention of the speaker. Hence, we can't shrug off the role of non-verbal speech act in our communication.

The importance of non-verbal speech act was well recognized by Austin. He has used the non-verbal speech act in his varied formulations. While describing the salient characteristics of explicit performative utterance, Austin argues that it contains the *tone of voice, cadence, gesture, the nature of circumstances* in which an utterance is used. For instance, Austin writes, "We may accompany the utterance of words by gesture (Winks, pointings, shruggings, frowns, & C) or by ceremonial non-verbal actions. These may sometimes serve without utterance of any words, and their importance is very obvious."[10] He also conceives as to the explicit performative utterances are like non-linguistic action *vis-à-vis* linguistic action. "The situation in the case of actions which are non-linguistic but similar to performative utterance........"[11] Likewise, when

Austin elucidates the illocutionary acts, he remarks, "Acts of both kinds can be performed—or, more accurately, acts called by same name (for example, acts equivalent to the illocutionary act of the warning or the perlocutionary act on convincing)—can be brought of non-verbally."[12] Indeed, Austin didn't brush aside the role of non-verbal act. However, he could not develop it in the existing domain of philosophy of language due to his premature death.

## REFERENCES

1. Searle, J.R. (1979): *Expressions and Meaning*, pp. 31-32.
2. *Ibid.*, p. 32
3. *Ken Upaniṣad*, 1-4 to 8.
4. *Ibid.*, 2-3.
5. *Mundak Upaniṣad*, 3-2-9.
6. Bhartṛhari: *Vākyapadīya*, Part I, 134 (142).
7. Quoted from Iyer, K.A. Subramanian (1969): *Bhartṛhari, 'A Study of Vākyapadīya' in the light of ancient commentaries*, p. 144.
8. *Ibid.*, p. 67.
9. Quoted from Pandey, K.C. (1969): *Abhinavagupta: An Historical and Philosophical Study*, p. 47.
10. Austin, J.L. (1982): *How to Do Things with Words*, edited by J.O. Urmson and Marina Sbisa, p. 76.
11. *Ibid.*, p. 69.
12. *Ibid.*, p. 121.

# 7

# How Performatives Exactly Work

Language is the medium of communication. However, the most critical question is: how language works? Some eminent contemporary philosophers have argued either in favour of standardization or conventionalization, as down to earth touchstones facilitating the functioning of language. Secondly, when the speaker uses any utterance, does the hearer directly or indirectly infer its performativity?

Austin delineated the nature of utterance in his celebrated book *How to Do Things With Words* (1962). He made a clear cut distinction between the constative and the performative utterances by virtue of description and action, respectively. Later on, he himself disowned this distinction and purported that *every speech is an act*. In other words, an utterance not only informs or describes something but also performs some act which is known as speech act theory. By and large, there is no controversy about this issue.

The philosophers, who express their agreement about Austin's doctrine solely consider this problem in the context of the hearer's perspectives. This approach, however, ignores an indispensable dimension of an utterance, like *the intention of the speaker*, which has a major role in our communication. Lack of consideration of intention causes communication gap between the speaker and the hearer. Although, an utterance is both constative and performative nonetheless on the basis of the speaker's intention, one can plainly distinguish between the two aspects. A speaker does not always use a performative sentence for doing something, sometimes he simply wants to inform the hearer or listener. For instance, at the end of a ceremony, someone announces: this was the best arrangement. Of course, this utterance may be simply informative or it may be a sort of stimulation for others to arrange such sort of ceremony. The meaning of utterances relies upon the judgment of the hearer and his interpretation of the intention of the speaker. If we ignore the speaker's intention, we will not be able to judge the actual meaning of this utterance. In my article, *Why to distinguish performative and constätive utterances?*, I have argued,

> "Thus, the intention of the speaker is critically important in understanding the meaning of utterances. Merely knowledge of the context in which an utterance takes place may not be adequate in understanding the meaning assigned by the speaker. The hearer also attempts to make inference regarding intention of the speaker."[1]

Later on, Searle discussed the problems of *how performatives work* in the light of *self-guaranteeing* and *self-referential* characters. While considering the self-guaranteeing character, he raised a crucial question: Why is it possible as to in some cases, the performative utterance can't be lie or mistaken or false while some utterances, it can be lie or mistaken or false. For instance, Ram promises to come and see you next week, this utterance may be false or mistaken. Whereas, when we say, I promise to come and see you next week, this utterance can't be false or mistaken. Searle pretended that when we say, I promise to come and see you next week, we emphasise on the force of utterance, *i.e.*, utterance of the sentence and its literal meaning both are identical. Searle called it *self-guaranteeing* character of an utterance.

Searle further defined *self-referential* character in terms of the word *hereby*. When a person, for example, utters, I *hereby* promise to do so and so, he does not describe or report about his promise. Indeed, he promises or he guarantees about his promises which betoken the real intention of the speaker. Otherwise, an utterance may be confused between actual intention and hidden intention. Searle, therefore, introduced *hereby* as a useful touchstone, which reveals the self-referential character of the performative. By virtue of the word *hereby*, he, therefore, distinguished between the constative and the performative utterance. Constative utterance underlies merely its literal meaning. However, when we use the word *hereby*, the utterance is treated as performative utterance to the extent that it not only includes its literal meaning but also speaker's intention, as Searle wrote:

> "Performative speaker meaning includes sentence meaning but goes beyond it. In the case of the performative utterance, the intention is that the utterance should constitute the performance of the act named by the verb. The word 'hereby' makes this explicit, and with the addition of this word, sentence meaning and performative speaker meaning coincide."[2]

Searle endeavoured to make a clear-cut distinction between the constative and the performative utterance by virtue of the word *hereby* which is problematic. Firstly, *hereby* is not common language, it is an official language. It has been used in the various offices for various legal proceedings. Secondly, it must demand some written documents. In our conversational talk, therefore, this word may not be used, and if it were used, it would be redundant. Thirdly, the word 'hereby' has always been used for continuing the processing, discussed prior. Fourthly, even if a speaker uses the word 'hereby' notwithstanding his intention may be confused between actual and hidden intention. Instead, without using the word 'hereby', a speaker may express his real intention. It rests upon speaker's personality, sincerity, character, nature and so forth. If the speaker is sincere, he must express his real intention. At that juncture, it is meaningless to consider whether the word 'hereby' was used or not. Moreover, if the speaker is insincere and cunning then in spite of using the word 'hereby', he may actually hide his real intention and report a hidden intention, making task of the hearer much more difficult. 'Hereby', therefore, would not be an appropriate touchstone for deciding the actual and hidden intention. Fifthly, 'hereby' may be a sort of information or description. For example, I hereby inform that professor X is appointed as a vice-chancellor of Allahabad University. This utterance is plainly informative. In the light of the above discussion, we may say that 'hereby' is not an accurate criterion for deciding the character of the performatives.

Likewise, when Searle discussed the self-guaranteeing character of an utterance, he emphasised on the *force* of an utterance which contains that utterance of the sentence and its literal meaning both are identical. For example, I promise to do so and so. Of course, when the speaker uses the word 'I........', then he emphasises on the force of the utterance, and it would be awry to say that we emphasise on something with insincerity. Although, Searle's contention appears correct, at first glance nonetheless he did not discuss an inevitable dimension of communication, like the speaker's personality, *i.e.*, the speaker is sincere or insincere, honest or dishonest and the like. If the speaker is sincere and honest, indeed his intention and force would be identical even if he uses the utterance in the third person. Whereas, when the speaker is insincere and dishonest, he uses an utterance even in the first person nonetheless it would not be the performative inasmuch as the speaker may hide his real intention and express hidden intention. We, therefore, argue that even self-guaranteeing character would not be an appropriate criterion for the performatives. Thus, the only way for deciding the constative and the performative is *the intention of the speaker*.

However, it is important to mention that when an utterance is used with conformity in a certain convention, the role of intention of the speaker is retrenched in communication. Although, the speaker's intention may be wrong nevertheless the act must be performed. For example, in the law court, in front of the Registrar, a man asserts looking at a woman that I do you my lawful wedded spouse. In such circumstances, merely utterance of certain words is adequate for the successful performative and in this regard the question of the intention of the speaker is meaningless. Likewise, on the occasion of inauguration of the seminar, the chairperson of the seminar announces as to I inaugurate this seminar. This utterance must perform the act of inauguration and what is the intention of the speaker, is irrelevant. While, in the absence of conventionalization, the intention of the speaker plays a major role in communication between the speaker and the hearer. In such circumstances, there are no norms, whereby, the hearer may succeed to judge the real intention of the speaker. He, therefore, indirectly endeavours to infer the real intention of the speaker by Gricean mechanism. Apparently, *convention does not reflect the intention and intention may not be easily revealed by convention.* In this regard, we may say as to Searle's contention is untenable because he emphasises too much in favour of the intention of the speaker, even in the case of convention, as he wrote:

> "A special convention that certain literal sentences of natural languages count as the performances of a certain declarations within the institution. The intention by the speaker in the utterance of those sentences that his utterance has a declarational status, that it creates a fact corresponding to the propositional content."[3]

Searle, furthermore, purported that performative utterance must be overt and explicit:

> "There are a number of semantic features which block a performative occurrence. So for example, famously, *'hint' 'insinuate'* and *'boast'* can't be used performatively, because they imply that the act was performed in a way that was not explicit and overt, and performative utterances are completely explicit and overt."[4]

However, Searle's contention creates a controversy. On the one hand, Searle emphasises that performative utterances must be explicit and overt; on the other hand, he advocates on the force of utterance, *i.e.*, the self-guaranteeing character. The question is: *Is the force of an utterance explicit and overt*? Obviously, there are several cases, wherein it is very difficult to chalk out where the force of an utterance is? For example, *have you purchased this horse in ten thousand rupees?* On the variations of its force or emphasis, its meanings may change. Although this utterance sounds like a *question*, however, with variation of emphasis on different fragment or word of this utterance, its meaning does change. When emphasis is on *have you* its meaning would be that you can't purchase this horse because this is beyond your income or status. Here, the intention of the hearer would be sarcastic. The speaker does not think that the horse is really purchased by the person, who is being addressed. Again, when emphasis is on *this horse*, its meaning would be as to this horse is vicious, weak or not competent to serve the purpose of the buyer. Likewise, when emphasis is on *ten thousand*, its meaning would be that this amount is too much for this horse. Furthermore, when emphasis is put on *purchase*, its meaning would be that you have not purchased this horse. It may even imply that you have stolen or hired this horse for some time and so forth. Indeed, the context of utterance, the intention of the speaker, variations in emphasis on certain words of utterances seems to be the most important factor for determining the meaning of a sentence. Thus, the variation of pitch, intonation, and cadence of the utterance make different meanings of the utterance. So far as, this utterance must be performative nonetheless it is hard to decide where the force in this utterance is.

Likewise, all sorts of indirect speech act must be performative. Searle himself uttered,

> "In indirect speech acts the speaker communicates to the hearer more than he actually says by way of relying on their mutually shared background information, both linguistic and non-linguistic.... Many confusions in recent moral philosophy rest on a failure to understand the nature of such indirect speech acts."[5]

However, its form is not very clear and overt. Suppose, someone asks his son, do you know how much is the telephone bill? This utterance is a sort of indirect speech act. However, what does he want to say by this utterance, is not very obvious. By and large, this utterance appears like a question *i.e.*, the father would like to know about telephone bill. Besides, it may be possible that the father indirectly instructs his son to avoid unnecessary calls, on account of too much telephone bill. Indirect speech act, therefore, is not very clear and overt; however, its performativity is undoubted.

Similarly, all sorts of non-verbal speech acts are performative. For example, Austin claimed,

> "We may accompany the utterance of the words by gesture (winks, pointings, shruggings, frowns & C) or by ceremonial non-verbal actions. These may sometimes serve without the utterance of any words and their importance is very obvious."[6] Again, "The situation in the case of actions which are non-linguistic but similar to performative utterances........"[7]

However, it is very difficult to judge its performativity. For example, if someone asks you about anything but you don't speak and remain silent. What would you like to communicate by your silence? It is not an easy task for the hearer to judge. Its meaning may be that you would like to ignore this question; it may be that your question is irrelevant in this context; you may express your agreement and disagreement by your silence; apart from this, it may even be possible as to the answer of this question is indescribable to the extent that it is beyond our mind, intellect and language, so we can't say anything at all regarding our question.

Furthermore, for successful communication, the intention of the speaker is very important. However, it is also very difficult to infer the intention of the speaker. Intention may be confused between actual and hidden intention. More precisely, intention is subjective, lacking objective way to judge it and therefore, nobody can provide any clear-cut touchstones for inferring it. Even a speaker may assert that he is telling his very intention, however, he may actually hide his real intention and report a hidden intention.

*All the four sorts of utterances, therefore, must be performatives nonetheless its performativity is not very clear and overt. In so far as, these are not only bound up with the speaker but also with the hearer's personality, talent, calibre, subtle and extensive thinking and also his skill. If hearer is very dull and layman, there is the least possibility that he would succeed to identify their performativity.* So, it would not be appropriate to pretend that whether performative utterances are explicit and overt?

Later on, Searle endeavoured to distinguish between *linguistic declaration* and *extra-linguistic declaration* by virtue of semantic property. Linguistic declaration creates a linguistic fact like, promise, order and so forth. Whereas, extra-linguistic declaration creates an extra linguistic fact, *i.e.,* it must perform some act in actual world *vis-à-vis* merely saying something, for example, adjourning the meeting, declaring wars and so forth. Well, Searle claimed that there are some utterances, which literal utterance is adequate in itself because "language is itself an institution."[8] It quite likely implies that these utterances do not perform any sort of act in the actual world, except saying something. Thus, they work between *word to word* and not *word to world.* Instead, there are enormous utterances which literal utterance is inadequate in itself. In other words, their success relies upon the performance of some act in the actual world. They, therefore, work between *words to world, not only word to word.*

The above distinction is untenable. Every utterance is bound up with action rather than limited to its literal meaning. For example, Searle purported that 'I promise', it does not create any extra-linguistic fact. However, the question is: May 'I promise' by saying literally that 'I promise'. Of course, 'I promise' must insinuate some action, *i.e.* promise about something. Suppose, we utter that 'I promise' to come and see you next week but my intention may not be fair and vehemently, I would not like to meet you. In those circumstances, we may not say that I have promised. Secondly, if we suppose that this utterance does not create any extra-linguistic fact then the second part of this utterance, *i.e. come and see you next week* would be redundant which is incorrect. Likewise, I *order you to leave the room.* However, the question is what sort of order? Indeed, *order is bound up with 'leave the room'*, which is not merely literal but also actual. We, therefore, can't lay down that language is in itself an institution and its literal utterance is adequate, *per se.* Instead, we may distinguish between linguistic and extra-linguistic declaration, regarding following grounds:

- Extra-linguistic declaration directly bound up with action whereas linguistic declaration does it indirectly.
- The former is past-oriented while the later is future-oriented. Searle's puzzle is, therefore, unnecessary when he utters,

> "........how could any verbs have such remarkable properties just as a matter of semantics? I can't fix the roof by saying, "I fix the roof" and I can't fry an egg by saying, "I fry an egg," but I can promise to come and see you just by saying, "I promise to come and see you" and I can order you to leave the room just by saying, "I order you to leave the room". Now, why the one and not the other?"[9]

Another crucial question is: *Whether the hearer directly or indirectly infers the speech act? viz.*, the performative sentence is direct speech act or indirect speech act. A group of philosophers like *Lewis, Genet, Bach* and *Harnish* pretended that an utterance is primarily statement and the hearer indirectly infers its performativity by Gricean mechanism. Performative utterances are, therefore, treated as an indirect speech act. If someone utters, for example, can you pass the salt? the speaker is indirectly requesting to pass the salt. The hearer directly uptakes it as a statement, and indirectly, he judges its performativity. Likewise, when a person comes from outside and alleges, I feel suffocation in this room. This utterance directly is a statement and indirectly it is a performative inasmuch as the speaker wants to open the doors and windows of this room. These utterances are, therefore, directly a statement and indirectly performatives. As Bach and Harnish argued:

> "On our account, a performative sentence when used performatively is used literally, directly to make a statement and indirectly to perform the further speech act

> of the type (an order, say) named by the performative verb ('order')...... In our view, the performative formula is but one of a wide variety of forms of words which have become standardized for specific indirect uses, forms which serve to streamline or compress the audience's inference process. Familiar examples include "Can you......?," "I'd like you to ......" and "It would be nice if you would ......", not to mention a hedged performative like "I must ask you......", each standardly used to make a request indirectly."[10]

They, therefore, defined performative utterances as standardized indirect speech acts. Obviously, there are two specific terms Standardization and Indirection. While defining the Standardization, Bach and Harnish wrote,

> "...... (sentence form) T is standardly used to F in group G if and only if: (i) It is mutually believed in G that generally when a member of G utters T, his illocutionary intend is to F, and (ii) Generally when a member of G utters T in a context in which it would violate the conversational presumptions to utter T with (merely) its literally determined force, his illocutionary intend is to F."[11]

With regard to the above definition, an utterance may be used standardly; firstly, when it is rested upon *mutual belief* between the speaker and the hearer in a certain context. Secondly, it must avoid the *conversational presumptions*. For example, *'I order you to leave the room'*. Firstly, here the word 'order' has always been used for *order* by English speakers to the extent that it is rested upon mutual belief. And secondly, it also ignores the conversational presumption and therefore it must be treated as an order. Whereas, indirection means, an utterance is a direct statement and indirect speech act.

Later, Searle admitted that he thought like most of his colleagues for many years. He, however, changed his position when he observed certain problems in this argument. "The mistake is that the argument confuses being committed to having an intention with actually *having the intention.*"[12] Suppose, if a person utters 'I promise to come and see you next week' it may be possible that he made his promise insincerely and there are no such criteria which plainly distinguish between actual intention and expressed intention. Expressed intention may not be actual intention of any person while for successful communication, actual intention is inevitable. Searle, therefore, argued that we can't derive the performative form a statement. A statement or an assertion does not guarantee the actual intention of any speaker. However, when an assertion is self-referential, it must indicate assurance of actual intention. As he argued:

> "I have come to the unfortunate conclusion that any attempt to derive performatives from assertives is doomed to failure because assertives fail to produce the self-guaranteeing feature of performatives, and in failing to account for the self-guaranteeing feature, the analysis fails to account for performativity."[13]

Accordingly, Searle has shown that the performative is primarily speech act and an assertion bound up with such an utterance is derived from it.

Kent Bach and R.M. Harnish, later, refuted Searle's contention that there are differences between actual intention and expressed intention or hidden intention. "But there is no question about his being sincere in the communicative intention itself—what one can be insincere about is actually having the attitude one is expressing."[14] They, further, argued that a speaker firstly thinks and then he expresses it in words. It is not correct as to a speaker firstly speaks and then he thinks, whatever, he spoke. The distinction between actual and hidden intention is, therefore, blurred. As they admitted, "As Humpty Dumpty evidently appreciated, you choose your words to fit your intention, not your intention to fit your words."[15] However, when we ponder over the above discussion, we observe some mistake in Bach and Harnish's contention. Although, Bach and Harnish's endorsement is uncontroversial that a person firstly thinks and then he expresses it, in appropriate language and not *vice versa. Our thinking, however, may be distinguished between actual thinking and hidden thinking. A person may hide his actual thinking and report his hidden thinking and there is nothing wrong in it.* For example, I promise to do so and so, however my actual thinking may not be do so and so. Thus, it is not appropriate to say that intention may not be confused between actual intention and hidden intention.

Moreover, Bach and Harnish argued that an utterance is primarily a statement and speech act indirectly derives from it. It is argued that the seminal point of an utterance is *securing uptake*, implying that the hearer must understand the speaker's intention. If securing uptake is indispensable then the question is, *"Does the hearer uptake speech act, indirectly?"* So far as the hearer uptakes those things, which are inevitable for his job, *viz.*, hearer's job is to achieve his goal whatever, the speaker expresses by his utterance. At that juncture, it would be redundant to argue that the hearer firstly uptakes it as a statement and then he indirectly infers its performativity by Gricean mechanism. For instance, if the landlord of the house commands his renter that I order you to leave this house then the rentier *ipso facto* uptakes it as an order. He does not think that primarily this is a statement and indirectly he infers its performativity, *i.e.*, order which is the seminal point of this utterance, not only from the speaker's point of view but also from the hearer's point of view.

Secondly, if we conceived that an utterance is a direct statement and indirect speech act then on what ground, we will be able to distinguish between direct speech act and indirect speech act. For example, we may consider on a couple of utterances; Firstly, I order you to leave the room and secondly, I feel suffocation in this room. Superficially, both utterances appear similar. However, when we consider it subtly, we may say that the former instance is a sort of direct speech act, while the latter instance is a sort of indirect speech act. Whereas, on account of Bach and Harnish's contention, both instances would be a sort of indirect speech act to the extent that the hearer indirectly infers it performativity. The dichotomy between direct speech act and indirect speech act is, therefore, blurred and it would be more difficult for the hearer to judge; whether this utterance is direct speech act or indirect speech act.

Moreover, if every meaningful utterance is a statement, then it would be redundant to think that primarily this is a statement and then it is a performative. Regarding this issue, we may argue that by virtue of *Occam's razor or law of parsimony*, we should not consider irrelevant things, which are not inevitable for our jobs. By and large, an utterance is treated by the hearer as speech act. However, sometimes, it may fail to give concrete result in accordance with inwardness feature and then the hearer indirectly endeavours to judge its performativity. Thus, they treated as an indirect speech act. In addition, there are a number of utterances which directly behave like indirect speech act, for example, '*can you pass the salt?* It would be nice....', and so forth, which are known as indirect speech act.

Bach further attempted to make a nuance distinction between hedged performatives and embedded performatives on the basis of certainty which must be inherent with the intention of the speaker. By and large, when a person utters something in the normal sense then it does not force the hearer to perform the act regarding this utterance. Moreover, when the speaker utters something forcefully then it does not endow with any sort of relaxation for the hearer, *i.e.*, it must underlie compulsion or certainty for the hearer to do as per the utterance. For instance, I order you to leave the room; this utterance has two dimensions; firstly, hedged performative like I order you to leave the room and embedded performative like I must order you to leave the room. Although, both utterances have plainly shown:

> ".....it is necessary for the speaker to order the hearer to leave. That is the belief the speaker is expressing in making the statement. Notice that in these cases this belief is distinct from the belief associated with the order itself, namely, the belief that the speaker is ordering the hearer to leave. The latter belief is not expressed, but it is implicated in the speaker's intention to be ordering."[16]

Well, on the one hand, Bach made a subtle distinction between hedged performative and embedded performative by virtue of the certainty or compulsion inasmuch as it must underlie the intention of the speaker. On the other hand, he emphasised on *standardization.* I think that both approaches are contradictory to each other and it would not be acceptable anyhow. In the case of standardization, speaker's intention is redundant. In such circumstances, language works as per certain norms which are objective and observable also. For example, in the law court, in front of the Registrar, someone signs on the written documents as 'I give and bequeath my house to my sister', at that place, the question of the intention of the speaker is meaningless. Even without intention, the act must be performed. Apparently, there is a standardized form of language which is used in various contexts and in accordance with contexts they must perform some acts. Indeed, this is not the characteristic of language, but it is the characteristic of standardization which is determined by society and culture. It does not mean that intention is not considerable or it is redundant. It may be considerable, in the absence of standardization. Apparently, in the absence of standardization language works as per intention of the speaker. Thus, standardization does not demand intention, *viz.*, it is adequate in itself to perform some acts. On this account, it would be untenable to distinguish between *hedged performatives* and *embedded performatives.* In the case of standardization, for example, the director of the institute utters that *you are hereby suspended.* This utterance does not provide any relaxation for the hearer to distinguish between hedged performative and embedded performative. It is quite likely implied that you must be suspended. The distinction between the hedged performatives and the embedded performatives is, therefore, not justifiable. However, it may be useful in the absence of standardization.

The above discussion highlights the fact that Bach and Harnish's contention as to performatives work as per standardized indirect speech act, is problematic. So far as I think, standardization and indirection both are contradictory to each other. In the case of standardization, which is rested upon *mutual belief* and *avoidance of conversational presumption*, as defined by Bach and Harnish, the hearer directly conceives the speech act. In the absence of standardization, however, the hearer endeavours to infer the intention of the speaker indirectly inasmuch as there are no standardized touchstones which facilitate the inference process. So, when Bach and Harnish pretended that even in the case of the standardization, the hearer indirectly infers the speech act. *It simply unfolds that even standardization is not very clear, viz., standardization is also confused, unclear, equivocal, complex, vague, and the like. The hearer, therefore, indirectly endeavours to take away this confusion by inference process.*

It does not imply that Searle's argument is appropriate, *i.e.*, an utterance is primarily performative and an assertion derives from it. This contention is also worth considerable from a certain point of view. Of course, in the presence of conventionalization, the hearer directly infers the speech act. Thus, an utterance is directly treated as a speech act. However, in the absence of conventionalization, performatives work regarding the intention of the speaker or mutual understanding between the speaker and the hearer. In these circumstances, an utterance is directly treated as an assertion or a statement and the hearer, indirectly infers the intention of the speaker. Thus, an utterance is direct statement and indirect speech act.

Various arguments presented in this paper identify conventionalization and standardization as two major dimensions for understanding the nature of performative utterances. The question of relative importance of conventionalization and standardization appears irrelevant. Standardization of performative utterance is a gradual process taking place in a socio-cultural context. By and large, conventionalized forms of performative utterances have been prevalently accepted and used. Later on, certain forms of conventional performative utterances acquire standardized form. Conventional performative utterances, therefore, evolve as standardized performative utterances. It may not be understood as to standardized performative utterances are perfect and ossify. The process of standardization of performative utterance is dynamic and continuous. When it has been used in our daily life, it becomes an indispensable fraction of conventionalization. Of course, conventionalization and standardization may not diametrically be converse aspects. Conventionalization underlies all sorts of standardization. It may not deem that conventionalization is ultimate, static and ossified. Socio-cultural contexts bestow strength and fecundity which facilitate the process of conventionalization and standardization. *Due to variation in socio-cultural contexts, convention may vary. The functioning of performatives is, therefore, relative to a socio-cultural context.* For example, I promise to do so and so, there may be a culture, wherein you can promise by saying merely that I promise while in the same culture, in case of conventionalization and standardization, *you can't promise by saying solely that I promise.* In such circumstances, you can promise, by signing some special legal documents only. Of course, the realm of standardization is very limited which indicate only formal and legal situations. The whole society, therefore, doesn't work as per the norms of standardization. Broadly, standardization is an aspect of conventionalization, whereas conventionalization relies upon socio-cultural contexts. We, therefore, conclude that performatives work as per socio-cultural contexts. Conventionalization and standardi-zation are embedded in the larger socio-cultural context to the extent that they become inseparable fragment of it.

Socio-cultural contexts, however, should not be taken as static and ossified. It is dynamic and continuous, like conventionalization and standardization. When a culture comes in contact with other culture, it leads to the process of *acculturation.* For example, when some persons of a culture interact with the person of another culture, they extensively observe nuances of the other culture and compare it with regard to their own culture. This process of acculturation leads to evolution of some novel values and norms, adopted by the person involved in such process. Gradually, these logical, rational and congruent novelties become an inevitable aspect of their culture and eventually, get adopted as a standardized form. These innovations through the medium of conventionalization are standardized. *The process of acculturation is unique and amenable for introducing dynamism in socio-cultural contexts.*

Another cardinal process of *ratiocination* also affects the socio-cultural contexts. In every culture, some person of intellectual class belongs to peer-groups. On the basis of logical and intellectual thinking, they dissent conservatism, fundamentalism and obscurantism, prevalent in their society. They, therefore, organize and participate in various intellectual discourses, meetings, seminars, etc., and argue against the fundamentalism inasmuch as, these are obstacles for the development of the society. While criticizing negative aspects of the society, they introduce some novel values and norms for its betterment. Although, fundamentalists always vehemently dissent such sort of innovations so that obscurantism continues in minds and actions of people. They fail to provide some logical argument in favour of obscurantism. They, therefore, endeavour to use and arouse emotions and feelings of masses, asserting that the founder of the society, *i.e.*, religious *Gurus* desire us to be like of obscurantism. They never accept that those norms may become irrelevant in the context of changing society and contemporary world. With the advent of information technology, the world is converting into a *global village*. In such circumstances, it is very difficult to abide by stereotypes of obscurantism which are noxious for the development of the society. So, majority of the people endeavour to adopt these innovations gradually and eventually it achieves the status of conventionalization and standardization, respectively. Such sort of societal phenomena may be observed even in contemporary society. Now-a-days, Pakistan and Afghanistan are good examples of such societal phenomena. Lately, Pakistani President General Parvez Musharruf proclaimed numerous reforms which conceive as a radical step towards the reform in Pakistan. Likewise, in Afghanistan, with the establishment of the new government, numerous traditional values which were imposed by fundamentalists are assuaged and replaced by some innovations. Apparently, performatives work as per socio-cultural contexts which may change with regard to acculturation. Conventionalization and standardization, therefore, must be deemed with reference to dynamic character of socio-cultural context.

However, in the absence of socio-cultural contexts of conventionalization and standardization, language may work as per following grounds. Firstly, *mutual understanding* between the speaker and the hearer may develop to facilitate functionality of a specific linguistic communication. Suppose two persons belonging to different cultures, meet each other. Obviously, their languages and cultures would be different. In such circumstances, they may not have common standardized and conventionalized form of language required for their communication. However, in such situation, they may evolve mutual understanding regarding language including signs, symbols etc. for their communication. Thus, mutual understanding is an outstanding phenomenon for communication.

Secondly, *job orientations* are also cardinal factor for performing the work in lack of conventionalization and standardization. Job orientation is bound up with common interest, goal and purpose. Thus, even if the speaker and the hearer differ in their calibre and mental status, however, due to similarities of job they succeed in communicating their ideas, without, ambiguity. In such circumstances, performatives work in accordance with the common purposes between the speaker and the hearer, *i.e., language works between words to work.*

Thirdly, in this regard, *hearer's motivation and propensity are unavoidable.* In several cases, it has been seen that the hearer uptakes the meaning of an utterance according to their propensity. For instance, when a person utters that we should not beat our wife. Obviously, regarding their propensity or motivation and even intellect, the hearers adopt it in various manners. Some persons may think that we should beat others, besides our wives while some other person may think that we should not beat anybody including our wives. Another example may be; someone of the family members utters that *it is Sunday today.* This utterance may be taken in various ways by varied family members depending upon their motivations. Firstly, someone may think that it is Sunday today, so we should go to the Church. Secondly, someone may think that today is holiday, so there is no hasty, *viz.,* we should take rest too much *vis-à-vis* other days. Thirdly, some others may think that *Kṛṣṇa* T.V. Serial will come today at 8.30 A.M. because, it is Sunday toḍay; while, if you have commenced a meeting on Sunday, then you will conceive uptake it in other manner.

Likewise, Upaniṣadik statement, *'Eko Brahman Dvitiyo Nāsti'* Śaṅkara interpreted it, Brahman is the only real and everything except Brahman is unreal, appearance, Māyā, Avidyā etc. On the basis of this interpretation, he propounded his noteworthy theory of non-dualism. Whereas, Rāmānuja interpreted this statement in different way. He argued that it does not mean that Brahman is the only real. Apart from Brahman, *Jīva* (*Chit*) and Matter (*Achit*) are also real, eternal and independent to each other, however, their existence rely upon God. It may imply that in addition to God, Chit and Achit are also real but these are not equivalent to God. God is substance while Chit and Achit are attributes of god. Rāmānuja, therefore, laid down his cardinal theory of Viśhiṣṭādvaita. Thus, the nature, propensity, motivation, etc. of the hearer are also very important for deciding the meanings. In addition, we can't disown the intention of the speaker, which we have discussed earlier, for successful communication.

Eventually, we may attempt to recapitulate our seminal ideas in foregoing discussion. Prevalently, performative sentences are directly treated as a speech act. Sometimes, it may fail to produce some consequential result regarding its inwardness then the hearer, indirectly endeavours to infer its performativity. These utterances are, therefore, treated as indirect speech act. Moreover, there may be some utterances, which are, naturally, indirect speech act. Secondly, performatives work as per socio-cultural contexts. Conventionalization and standardization are embedded in the larger socio-cultural context inasmuch as they become an inseparable fraction of it. However, in the absence of conventionalization and standardization, performatives work in accordance with following grounds:

- Mutual understanding between the speaker and the hearer.

- Job orientations among the person.
- Motivations and propensities of the hearer.
- The intention of the speaker.

## REFERENCES


1. Pandey, R.K. (2001): *Why to distinguish performative and constative utterances?* Indian Philosophical Quarterly, Vol. XXVIII No. 3. p. 361.
2. Searle, J.R. (1989): *How Performatives Work,* Linguistics and Philosophy, Vol. 12, p. 552.
3. *Ibid.*, p. 548.
4. *Ibid.*, p. 554.
5. Searle, J.R. (1979): *Expressions and Meaning,* pp. 31-32.
6. Austin, J.L. (1982): *How to Do Things with Words,* edited by J.O. Urmson and Marina Sbisa, p. 76.
7. *Ibid.*, p. 69.
8. Searle, J.R. (1989): *How Performatives Work,* Linguistics and Philosophy, Vol. 15, p. 98.
9. *Ibid.*, p. 535.
10. Bach, K. and Harnish, R.M. (1982): *How Performatives Really Work,* Linguistics and Philosophy, Vol. 15, p. 98.
11. Bach, K. and Harnish, R.M. (1979): *Linguistic Communication and Speech Acts,* M.I.T. Press, Cambridge, Mass, p. 19.
12. Searle, J.R. (1989): *How Performatives Work,* Linguistics and Philosophy Vol. 12, p. 546.
13. *Ibid.*, pp. 546-47.
14. Bach, K. and Harnish, R.M. (1982): *How Performatives Really Work,* Linguistics and Philosophy, Vol. 15 p. 96.
15. *Ibid.*, p. 105.
16. Bach, K. (1995): *Standardization* Vs. *Conventionalization,* Linguistics and Philosophy, Vol. 18. p. 680.

# 8

# Is Language ample *per se* for the Correct Inference of the Speaker's Intention?

Language is a vehicle to develop and communicate our ideas, thoughts and intentions. The role of perceived intention of the speaker by the hearer in communication is critically significant and it was first discussed by H.P. Grice. Grice in his article, *Meaning*, distinguishes between the *natural* and the *non-natural meaning*. On the one hand, the form of natural meaning is: x means that p and x means that p entails p (where, x is an object and p is a proposition). For instance, 'Those spots mean measles'; 'Those spots didn't mean anything to me, but to the doctor they mean measles'; 'The recent budget means that we shall have a hard year'. In these examples, each subject indicates a corresponding fact or it refers to something, like those spots indicating measles and recent budget indicating that...... Indeed, the meaning of these things are by and large conceived in all conventions in the same form. These examples are, therefore, clearly concerned with *natural meaning*.

The form of non-natural meaning, on the other hand, is: x means that p, and x means that p doesn't entails p. For instance, 'Those three rings of the bell (of the bus) mean that the 'bus is full' '. Precisely, the meaning of this utterance may not be similar in all conventions. In all likelihood, its meaning may vary in diverse conventions. In a certain convention, its meaning (*three rings of the bell*) may be that the *'bus is full'*. In some other convention, however, its meaning (three rings of the bell) may be conceived that the *'bus will stop'*. Hence, the meaning of this utterance may vary due to convention and the intention of the speaker. Grice called it *non-natural meaning* of an utterance.

Precisely, the *natural meaning* of an utterance hinges upon its *standard meaning* which is by and large similar in all conventions. While, the *non-natural meaning* of an utterance underpins over the *convention as well as the intention of the speaker* which varies due to person and contexts. Thus, there is no certainty in the non-natural meaning. While distinguishing between the natural and the non-natural meaning, Grice contended, "This question about the distinction between natural and non-natural meaning is, I think, what people are getting at when they display an interest in a distinction between "natural" and "conventional" signs. But I think my formulation is better. For some things which can mean$_{NN}$ something are not *signs* (*e.g.*, words are not), and some are not *conventional* in any ordinary sense (*e.g.*, certain gestures); while somethings which mean naturally are not signs of what they mean (*cf.* the recent budget example)."[1]

By virtue of this, Grice makes a clear-cut distinction in the following expressions, like *'means'*, *'means something'*, and *'means that'*. He conceived that when these expressions are used in the first set of examples (those spots mean that measles..., the recent budget....), it is concerned with natural meaning. Whereas, when these expressions are used in the second set of example (those three rings....), it is concerned with non-natural meaning.

Grice openly acknowledges that while distinguishing the natural and non-natural meaning, he was greatly impressed by C.L. Stevenson. In his book, *Ethics and Language* (1944), Stevenson advocated that whenever the speaker would like to communicate something, he/she intended to produce a tendency or attitude in the hearer and this tendency or attitude hinges upon, "*.......an elaborate process of conditioning attending the use of sign in communication.*"[2] Apparently, there are two ingredients of this definition. Firstly, *'an elaborate process of conditioning'* and secondly, *'attending the use of sign in communication'*. The former is concerned with *literal meaning*, which a person learnt by training leads to socio-cultural contexts. While, the later is bound up with *the intention of the speaker* which depends upon the uses of the sign, assigned by the speaker in a particular occasion. As Grice wrote, "No provision is made for dealing with statements about what a particular speaker or writer means by a sign on a particular occasion (which may well diverge from the *standard meaning* of the sign) ; nor is it obvious how the theory could be adopted to make such a provision. .........the causal theory ignores the fact that the meaning (in general) of a sign needs to be explained in terms of what users of the sign do (or should) mean by it on particular occasions and so the later notion, which is unexplained by the causal theory."[3] *The speaker's meaning is, therefore, different from the standard meaning.*

Grice emphasised on the second part of this definition and suggested that the meaning of an utterance underpins over the intention of the speaker along with its recognition by the hearer. When a person says something, he/she would like to communicate his/her intention. However, if the hearer doesn't recognise his/her intention, the speaker will not succeed in his/her aim. On this account, Grice emphasises on both 'the intention of the speaker' as well as its 'recognition by the hearer' for successful communication. As Grice asserts, " 'A $\text{meant}_{NN}$ something by x' is roughly equivalent to 'A uttered x with the intention of inducing a belief by means of the recognition of this intention."[4] It reveals that the sentence meaning of an utterance hinges upon the speaker's meaning and the speaker's meaning relies upon the speaker's intention. Thus, the sentence meaning eventually underpins over the speaker's intention.

**Sentence meaning → Speaker's meaning → Speaker's intention**

The question is: if the sentence meaning depends upon the speaker's meaning, then how the hearer will be able to judge the speaker's intention? Grice conceived that speaker's intention may be both overt or hidden. If the speaker's intention is overt then there will be no problem in judging its meaning. For instance, the speaker A is saying x and if he declares that he is using this utterance in that sense then the hearer will clearly narrow down the meaning assigned by the speaker. As he wrote, "It will be a case where an utterance is accompanied or preceded by a conscious "plan", or explicit formulation of intention (*e.g.*, I declare how I am going to use x, or ask myself how to "get something across"). The presence of such an explicit "plan" obviously counts fairly heavily in favour of the utterer's intention (meaning) being as 'planned'".[5]

Grice, however, raises a different issue. Suppose that while expressing his/her intention, a speaker uses a familiar expression in an unfamiliar way, then how will the hearer be able to judge his/her intention? According to Grice, in such a situation, the context will be only criterion to judge the actual meaning of an utterance. As he said, "Again, in cases where there is doubt, say, about which of two or more things an utterer intends to convey, we tend to refer to the context (linguistic or otherwise) of the utterance and ask which of the alternatives would be relevant to the other things he is saying or doing, or which intention in a particular situation would fit in with some purpose he obviously has (*e.g.*, a man who calls for a "pump" at a fire would not want a bicycle pump). Non-linguistic parallels are obvious: *context is* a criterion in settling the question of why a man who has just put a cigarette in his mouth has put his hand in his pocket;...."[6] He further explained, "....the criteria for judging the linguistic intentions are very like the criteria for judging the non-linguistic intentions is to show that linguistic intentions are very like non-linguistic intentions."[7]

Here, it is important to mention that Alexander Millar argued that Grice emphasised on both *intention* as well as *convention* to judge the meaning of an utterance. As he wrote, "Thus, the notion of sentence-meaning is explained in terms of the notion of speaker's meaning and the notion of convention, where the notion of speaker's meaning is explained in terms of utterer's intention. This is why Grice's account is sometimes known as a *convention plus intention* account of sentence meaning."[8] However, it appears that Miller's argument is converse to Grice's formulation. Grice never emphasised on *convention* to judge the speaker's intention. Strictly speaking, he was against convention for deciding the non-natural meaning of an utterance. He himself holds that by and large someone understands that the distinction between the natural and non-natural meaning is *natural* and *conventional* respectively. While, as a ground reality, non-natural meaning is neither concerned with *convention* nor concerned with *sign*. Let us suppose that Grice conceived as to the speaker's intention is narrowed down by convention, then why Millar wrote that in Grice's formulation, "the meaning of language is non-circularly analyzed in terms of mental content."[9] Well, if Millar, on the one hand, conceived that speaker's meaning is deduced by mental content, then why, on the other hand, he emphasised on convention. Indeed, both of the things, *i.e.*, *convention* and *mental content* are contradictory to each other. If meaning is determined by convention, then the role of mental content is diminished. And when meaning is determined by mental content then what is the need of convention? So far as I understand, Grice emphasised on the speaker's intention *vis-à-vis* convention. Grice himself wrote, '....the distinction between natural and non natural meaning is, I think, what people are getting at when they display an interest in a distinction between "natural" and "conventional" signs. But I think my formulation is better. For somethings which can $mean_{NN}$ something are not *signs* (*e.g.*, words are not), and some are not *conventional* in any ordinary sense)....' It seems that Millar did not contemplate on this passage. It will be interesting to mention that J.R. Searle (but not Grice), in his article, *'What is Speech Act?'* advocated on both intention and convention.

Paul Ziff, in his article, *On H.P. Grice's account of meaning*, produced counter example against Grice's contention. In his counter example, he tried to show that neither speaker's intention nor hearer's recognition is important for communication. Ziff said, "On being inducted into the army, George is compelled to take a test designed to establish sanity. George is known to be an irritable academic. The test he is being given would be appropriate for morons. One of the questions asked is: 'What would you say if you were asked to identify yourself?' George replied to the officer asking the question by uttering (3):

**(3) Ugh ugh blugh blugh ugh blug blug."[10]**

While saying this, George intended to offend the officer and he wanted to offend the officer in the sense that the officer must recognise his intention. But the officer doesn't recognise his intention and thereby he refuses to be offend. Precisely, in this sense, the intended effect is somehow within the control of the audience. Hence, according to Grice's analysis, George means$_{NN}$ something by (3). But according to Ziff, George doesn't mean anything by (3). By virtue of this, Ziff endeavoured to prove that the role of the intention of the speaker is retrenched in communication.

The question is: what device would be helpful to narrow down the meaning of an utterance in such a situation? In this regard, Ziff considered on varied factors, for instance, *the use of the expression and its relation to other sentences, sounds, the statement of a 'regularity'*, and so forth. As he said, "To be concerned with what people intend (or would intend) to effect by uttering an expression is to be concerned with the use of the expression..... the use of an expression is determined by many factors, many of which have nothing (or have nothing directly) to do with the meaning: acoustic shape is one such factor, length another...... The syntactic and the semantic structure of any natural language is essentially recursive in character. What any given sentence means depends on what (various) other sentences in the language mean."[11] He moreover suggested, "That people generally intend (or would intend) this or that by uttering an utterance has, at best, as much significance as a statement to the effect that when 'Pass the salt!' is uttered, generally people are eating, thus what I have elsewhere called the statement of a 'regularity'. Not all regularities are semantically relevant: a regularity couched in terms of people's 'intentions' is not likely to be.....But even if such regularities were somehow relevant, that would not matter much. A regularity is no more than a ladder which one climbs and then kicks away."[12]

J.R. Searle also presented another counter example, "Suppose that I am an American soldier in the Second World War and I am captured by Italian troops. And suppose also that I wish to get these troops to believe that I am a German officer in order to get them to release me. What I would like to do is to tell them in German or Italian that I am a German officer. But let us suppose I don't know enough German or Italian to do that. So I, as it were, attempt to put on a show of telling them that I am a German officer by reciting those few bits of German that I know, trusting that they don't know enough German to see through my plan. Let us suppose that I know only one line of German, which I remember from a poem I had to memorise in a high school German course. Therefore, I a captured American, address my Italian captors with the following sentence: 'Kennst dud as Land, wo die Zitronen blühen?'"[13]

On the basis of this utterance, Searle attempted to show that albeit an American soldier I intend to produce a certain effect, especially the effect to believe that I am a German officer, so that I want to create this belief by saying in German language and I also want that my intention should be recognized by German officer. But German officers don't recognise my intention to the extent that in German language, this utterance, *i.e.*, 'Kennst dud as Land, wo die Zitronen blühen?', is conventionally used for different purpose, so that naturally this utterance 'Kennst dud as Land, wo die Zitronen blühen?' doesn't mean that I am a German officer as desired by an American soldier. By virtue of this, Searle endeavoured to justify that merely intention is not enough for communication. In addition to *intention, convention* is also an important facet to narrow down the meaning of an utterance.

While considering this, Searle remarks, "Grice's account can be amended to deal with counter-examples of this kind. We have here a case where I am trying to produce a certain effect by means of the recognition of my intention to produce that effect, but the device I use to produce this effect is one which is conventionally, by the rules governing the use of that device used as a means of producing quite different illocutionary effect. We must therefore reformulate the Gricean account of meaning in such a way as to make it clear that one's meaning something when one says something is more than just contingently related to what the sentence means in the language one is speaking. In our analysis of illocutionary acts, we must capture both the *intentional* and the *conventional* aspects and especially the relationship between them. In the performance of an illocutionary act, the speaker intends to produce a certain effect by means of getting the hearer to recognize to produced that effect, and furthermore, if he is using world literally, he intends this recognition to be achieved in virtue of the fact that the rules of using this expressions with the production of that effect."[14] Searle's view can be schematized thus:

**Sentence meaning → Speaker's meaning → Speaker's intention + Convention**

Apparently, Searle conceived both intention and convention for successful communication *viz.*, meaning is not only determined by intention but also by its convention. However, it seems that Searle's contention is also untenable. When the speaker uses an utterance, the hearer endeavours to narrow down its meaning by the rules of conventions embedded in various forms in different societies. However, if performatives work by the rules of society then the role of *the intention of the speaker* is diminished. It reveals that there is no need to judge the intention of the speaker in a certain convention.

In addition to this, when emphasis is laid on the intention then it is not necessary that the intention of the speaker may be in accordance with convention. If *intention* and *convention* both are symmetrical, then there is no need to judge the speaker's intention to the extent that language works as per the rules of convention. Intention, however, becomes important when there are no certain norms. The hearer, therefore, endeavours to extract its meaning by Gricean Mechanism. Elsewhere the author has stated: "However, it is important to mention that when an utterance is used in conformity with certain convention, the role of the intention of the speaker's is retrenched in communication. Although, the speaker's intention may be wrong, nevertheless, the act must be performed. For example, in the law court, in front of the registrar, a man asserts looking at a woman that *I do you my lawful wedded spouse*. In such circumstances, merely utterance of certain words is adequate for successful performative and in this regard, the question of the intention of the speaker of the intention is meaningless. ..........While, in the absence of the conventionalization, the intention of the speaker plays a major role in communication between the speaker and the hearer. In such circumstances, there are no norms by which, the hearer may succeed to judge the real intention of the speaker. He, therefore, indirectly endeavours to infer the intention of the speaker by Gricean mechanism. Apparently, *convention does not reflect the intention and intention may not be easily revealed by convention."*[15]

Here it is important to mention that while comparing Grice's and Searle's contention, A. Millar argued that Searle's argument hinges upon the fallacy of circularity, while there is no circularity in Grice's contention. Millar wrote, "However, this shows that there is a problem with Searle's modified version of Grice's analysis. The problem is that the analysis now appears to be circular. Recall that Grice's central idea is that we can non-circularly define a notion of speaker's meaning in terms of speaker's intentions, and then non-circularily define the notion of sentence meaning in terms of speaker's meaning and convention. The result is suppose to be non-circular analysis of sentence meaning. *But the second condition introduced in Searle's modification seems to presuppose the notion of sentence meaning: that is, the speaker's meaning conventionally associated with token of a sentence-type.* This renders the account of sentence meaning circular: we define this in terms of speaker's meaning, the definition of which presupposes an account of sentence meaning. Is there any way Searle can respond to this charge of circularity?"[16]

In our view Millar's contention is not justifiable in respect of Searle's formulation. Searle never said that sentence meaning is defined in terms of speaker's meaning and speaker's meaning is defines in terms of sentence meaning. In his diverse formulations, Searle emphasised merely on speaker's intention, *i.e.*, intentionality as well as convention, but he never emphasised on sentence type. For instance, while emphasising on convention, Searle said, "The meaning of sentence is entirely a matter of conventions of the language. But sentences are tools to talk with. So even though language constrains speaker-meaning, speaker meaning is still the primary form of linguistic meaning because the linguistic meaning of sentence functions to enable speaker's of the language to use sentences to mean something in utterances. The speaker's utterance meaning is primary notion of meaning for our purposes in analysing the function of language."[17] Likewise, while emphasising on intention, he remarked, "The intentionality of the mind not only creates the possibility of meaning, but it limits its form........Another aim, then, of the analysis of meaning is to show how the possibilities and limitations of meaning derive from the intentionality of the mind."[18] It appears that Millar could not pay attention on these contentions and on the basis of certain arguments he narrowed down a conclusion and claimed that 'Is there any way Searle can respond to this charge of circularity?'

Indeed, language is a device to express our thought, intention and so forth. The speaker, however, may use deception to hide his real intention in spoken language, *viz.*, sometimes he may succeed to hide his real intention and report a hidden intention, making the task of the hearer strenuous and intricate. This problem leads us to rethink that, *"Is spoken language adequate for the correct inference of the speaker's intention?"* In every walk of life, we frequently observe as to a person thinks something and utters something else. In other words, saying and doing are asymmetrical. In such circumstances, it would be inadequate to judge the meaning of a sentence on the basis of its literal meaning. In this regard, it is *sine qua non* to study not only the nature and applications of language but also its relation to intention and behaviour which may be broadly called *linguistic behaviour*. Apparently, intentions are expressed by language and behaviour both. There may be congruence or incongruence in intention, language and behaviour. It is suggested that congruence in the intention, language and behaviour must reveal the real intention of the speaker, which may be called *depth language* (as shown in diagram **A)**. Whereas, incongruence in the above three do not reveal the real intention of the speaker which may be called *surface language*. Surface language may be of two sorts. Firstly, language and behaviour are congruent, but they do not reflect our real intention (refer diagram **B**). Secondly, all of the three intentions, language and behaviour are incongruent (refer diagram **C**). Congruent and incongruent relationships in intention, language and behaviour are diagrammatically presented below:

**Depth Language**
**A**

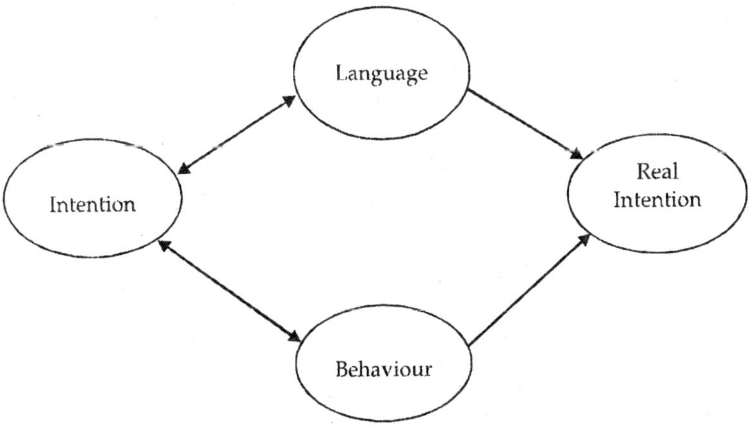


**Surface Language**
**B**

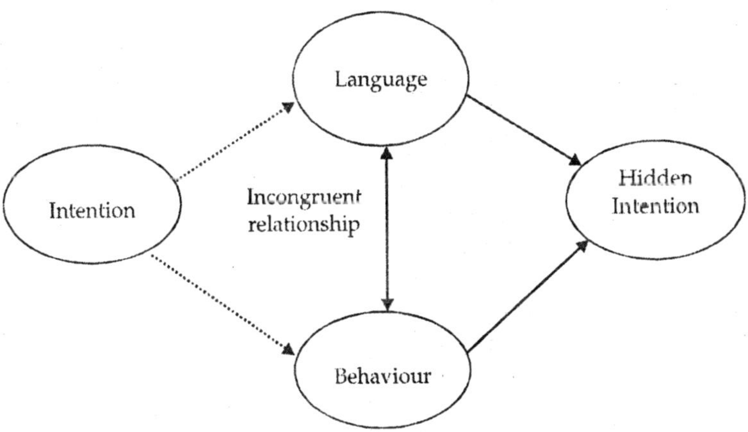

C

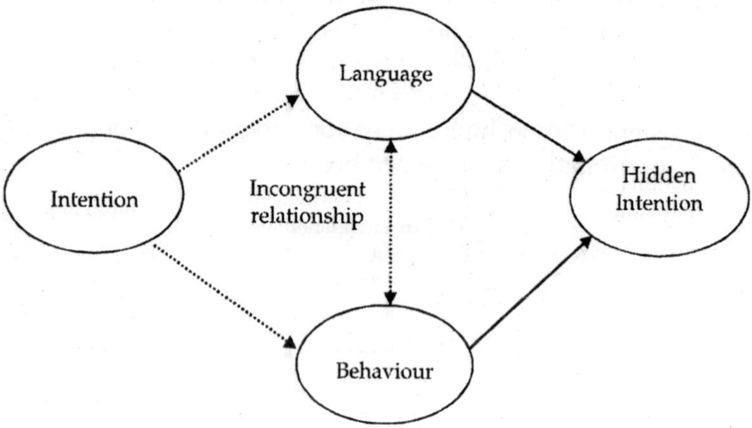


The surface language, therefore, does not reflect the real intention of the speaker. This leads to a question bound up with the hearer. Is it possible to know the real intention by hearing the spoken language or should the hearer infer the real intention by observing the behaviours of a person? In such a situation expressed behaviours of a person are more reliable indicators of the real intention *vis-à-vis* the spoken language to the extent that spoken language provides greater possibilities for hiding the real intention successfully. While, behaviours and acts may involve in really doing something indicating greater commitment of a person. Non-verbal behaviours are reflexive, natural and difficult for a person to hide across situations, unless one is trained in acting and consciously doing it. Non-verbal behaviours, therefore, are significantly more dependable cues for inferring the real intentions and its related thoughts rather than the spoken language.

However, Mark Platts argued that behaviour would not be an ample criterion to judge the real intention of the speaker. "Utterer's intentions are not recognized by unfailing intuition, nor do acts of God figure large. It is perhaps possible that very simple intentions be detected quasi-behaviouristically; but for intentions of any fair degree of complexity, this is simply implausible, the behavioural guide being too inexact. Any explanation of how such intentions are recognized will inevitably rely upon the audience's recognition of the literal meaning of the sentence; that meaning is the route to the speaker's intention, the reverse journey usually being impossible."[19]

Apparently, when Platts contended that the intention of the speaker is judged by the literal meaning, he plainly disowns the doctrine of language-game. According to this doctrine, there are varied functions of language *viz.*, an utterance has been used in various contexts and acquires various meanings. It does not mean that an utterance used in any context acquires any meaning. The meaning of an utterance (word) somewhat varies around its core or fundamental meaning. For instance, if a person commands his servant for a watch, then its meaning may concern with various sorts of watch but not with a horse or, a box and so forth. The meaning of an utterance, therefore, revolves around its *core meaning*. However, force, pitch, intonation, cadence, the intention, the historical background and behaviour of the speaker performs major role for deciding the meaning of an utterance.

Moreover, when we hold that the intention of the speaker is judged by its literal meaning, then we patently overlook the distinction between *real intention* and *hidden intention*. Indeed, the real intention is revealed in the language. However, when the speaker hides his real intention and expresses his hidden intention, then merely literal meaning would not be adequate to judge the real intention of the speaker. In such a situation, the role of behaviour becomes more reliable device. One may hide his real intention in language, but it is the least possibility that one may hide it in behaviour also. Sometime, behaviour may be hidden. Therefore, for the correct inference of the behaviour, we may create a situation. Across situations, it would be very strenuous for an individual to hide repeatedly the real intention in behaviour.

Moreover, commenting upon Grice doctrine Mark Platts highlights this question, "On Grice's theory, sentence meaning is defined in terms of the intention with which the sentence is uttered, along perhaps, with the response standardly secured in an audience by that utterance. Now, as an account of the meanings of sentences in natural languages this will not do for a simple reason: the majority of such sentences, natural languages containing a enumerable infinity of sentences, will never be uttered. They will therefore not be uttered with any intentions, nor will their utterance induce any response in an audience. What then, can Grice say about these unuttered sentences."[20]

Well, Platts contention is correct that all sentences of natural languages are not intentional. However, Platts does not consider why all sentences of natural languages are not intentional. Actually, there is a difference between *thought* and *intention.* Firstly, both thought and intention are the *feature of the mind,* and thereby both are subjective; intention is more subjective and private rather than the thought. Whenever, a Professor of mathematics delivers his lecture in the classroom we can't say that he is delivering his intention. Likewise, if the thinker of any discipline is expressing his contributions among scholars then we can't say that this is his intention. We can only say that this is his thought. Secondly, intention is always *motivated* attempt to achieve certain objective affect, while thought is not motivated. Thirdly, a person may hide his/her intention but it is the least possibility that he/she may hide his/her thought too. Intention may be hidden while thought is always open and overt. Fourthly, intention is always *speaker oriented* while thought is more or less *hearer oriented.*

Language communicates our thought and 'reveals intention'. Hypothetical intention is, therefore, not expressed in language. It is always disguised. Thus, all sorts of intentions must be thoughts but not all sorts of thoughts are intentions. Solely those thoughts are intentions which are motivated. In this regard, Platts rightly argues that all expressions of natural languages are not intentional, either real or hypothetical. Grice used the term 'hypothetical intention' for inferring the meanings of unuttered sentences.

Again, M. Platts asks that if there is hypothetical intention, then what sorts of constraints decide the meanings of unuttered sentences? If we say that there are no constraints then "the meanings of unuttered sentences will be left completely indeterminate: they could mean anything, so they do mean nothing."[21] On this account, Platts contended that the meaning of unuttered sentences is constrained by its literal meaning. While emphasizing this, Platts remarks, "Generally the constraints upon hypothetical intentions with which a sentence can be uttered, and upon the audience's responses to such an utterances, is precisely the meaning of the sentences.......If this is correct, the attempt to define the meanings of unuttered sentences in terms of hypothetical intentions and responses is hopeless: for it presupposes a prior notion of sentence-meaning."[22]

Well, the meaning of unuttered sentences must be constraint by some factors. However, the constraints are not only literal meaning but also force, context, intention, behaviour of the speaker. While emphasizing the importance of non-verbal actions, Prof. R. Prasad, in his book *Regularity, Normativity and Rules of Language*, wrote, "Understanding the use of an expression also involves understanding the verbal rules of its use, its logical relations to other expressions, etc. These verbal factors may be said to constitute the verbal context against the above which may be said to constitute the non-verbal context. Attention must be paid to both the verbal and non-verbal contexts. But it seams obvious that the latter is more important than the former. If we consider only the verbal factors, we will not be able to decide whether the sentence in question expresses a request, order, or prediction. This is natural in view of the fact that language is used to help its users in the transactions of everyday life and the verbal rules of use are involved only to make it an effective tool."[23]

Here, it is important to mention that Blackburn in his book, *Spreading the Word*, highlighted that *training* may be useful criterion to judge the real intention of the speaker. As he wrote, "......nothing constraints a group.......accept their training and the way the find if natural to take that training."[24] Of course, trainings are useful criterion to judge the intention of the speaker. Trainings, however, vary due to variation of socio-cultural contexts. In such circumstances, the speaker will say something and the hearer will uptake it in some other ways regarding his trainings. The hearer is, therefore, unable to understand the real intention. Thus, sole training can't be an appropriate procedure to constrain the meaning of an utterance.

By and large, biases and prejudices are hindrance to judge the real intention of the speaker. So, for correct inference, firstly, we should become free from biases and prejudice and achieve a status of objectivity and then we should attentively listen to a speech and observe behaviours. If the person is really innocent then his language and behaviour will be congruent to each other. Incongruent relationship of language and behaviour reveals his hidden intention. Sometimes, even a congruent relationship of language and behaviour do not reflect the real intention. However, close in depth observation of overall personality of a person may facilitate knowing his hidden intention.

The problem: "How to judge real intention?" still remains elusive. The hearer is always motivated to know it. Probably, one depends on one's perception of nuances of others behaviours, *i.e.*, paralanguage, verbal and non-verbal languages until one develops certain level of confidence in making rightful attributions for intention of expressed behaviour and languages. Hence, the hearer as observer continue to perceiving someone in question across situations until the hearer acquires certain level of confidence in his/her attribution of the person's real intention, hidden behind his expressed language and behaviours.

## REFERENCES

1. Grice, H.P. (1957): *'Meaning'*, 'The Philosophical Review', LXVI, No 3, See, Joy F. Rosenberg and Charles Travis (Ed), (1971): *'Reading in the Philosophy of Language'*, p. 438.
2. Stevenson, C.L. (1944): *Ethics and Language*, p. 57.
3. Grice, H.P. (1957): *'Meaning'*, 'The Philosophical Review', LXVI, No 3, See, Joy F. Rosenberg and Charles Travis (Ed), (1971): *'Reading in the Philosophy of Language'*, p. 439.
4. *Ibid.*, p. 441.
5. *Ibid.*, p. 443.
6. *Ibid.*, pp. 443-44.
7. *Ibid.*, p. 444.

8. Millar, Alexander (2004): *Philosophy of Language*, p. 228.
9. *Ibid.*, p. 228.
10. Ziff, Paul. (1967): *On H.P. Grice's Account of Meaning*, Analysis XXVIII, No. 1, See, Joy F. Rosenberg and Charles Travis (Ed), (1971): *Reading in the Philosophy of Language*, p. 445.
11. *Ibid.*, pp. 449-50.
12. *Ibid.*, p. 450.
13. Searle, J.R. (1965): *What is Speech Act?* The Philosophy of Language, J.R. Searle (Ed.) pp. 45-46.
14. *Ibid.*, p. 46.
15. Pandey, R.K (2003): *How Peformatives Exactly Work*, Indian Philosophical Quarterly, Vol. XXX, No. 2, p. 223.
16. Millar, Alexander (2004): *Philosophy of Language*, p. 233.
17. Searle, J.R. (1999): *Mind Language and Society: Philosophy in the Real World*, Phoenix, p. 140.
18. Searle, J.R. (1983): *Intentionality: An essay in the philosophy of mind*, pp. 166-67.
19. Platts, M. (1979): *Ways of Meaning*, p. 91.
20. *Ibid.*, p. 89.
21. *Ibid.*, p. 89.
22. *Ibid.*, p. 90.
23. Prasad, R. (1989): *Regularity, Normativity and Rules of Language*, p. 3.
24. Blackburn, S. (1984): *Spreading the Word*, p. 128.

# Epilogue

Austin's Speech Act Theory, a major constituent in the development of analytical philosophy has a special place in the Contemporary Western Philosophy. The chapter of the book critically narrates evolution of the theory and its present status. Its various dimensions along with comments of eminent philosophers are discussed and new insights are presented highlighting the following:

- Distinction of the constative and the performative utterances.
- How language works in different socio-cultural contexts.
- The role of non-verbal language in communication.
- The intertwined relations of thought, language and behaviour.

At the outset of his book, *How to Do Thing with Words,* Austin presented a new canvass of language stating that a meaningful utterance may be of two sorts: the constative and the performative. The constative is used to say something while the performative is used to perform something and therefore, the former is in the from of true or false, while the latter is felicitous or infelicitous. Eventually, he concluded that this distinction is not justifiable. Austin, therefore, brushed aside this distinction and argued that *every speech is an act, i.e.,* an utterance not only describes or states something but also performs some act and he called it speech act theory.

The book argues that this formulation of Austin is not tenable. Well, at the surface, it seems that there is no distinction between the constative and the performative utterances.

However, nuances of observations of various facets lead us to think that this distinction is justified. Whenever, a speaker uses his/her language, the hearer without considering the speaker's intention, endeavours to narrow down the meaning underpinned over either lexical or literal meaning. This thing shrugs off the role of the intention of the speaker which performs a major role in communication. If we conceive that the speaker uses his/her utterance in both senses, the question of *the indeterminacy of meaning* would emerge. In such a situation, the speaker will say something and the hearer will fathom something else. It reveals that when the speaker uses his/her utterance, the hearer should concentrate not only on its lexical or literal meaning but also on the intention of the speaker.

Moreover, the issue *How language works?*, is further examined. Indeed, this is a controversial question for philosophers. J.R. Searle emphasised on conventionalization, while K. Bach and R.M. Hernish advocated for standardization. It is argued that language works in accordance with socio-cultural contexts. Conventionalization and standardization are embedded in the larger socio-cultural contexts. The question, however, becomes more intricate when two persons belonging to two different socio-cultural contexts, interact. Indeed, their socio-cultural conditions would influence their communication and their different background may cause problems in communication. On this account, I advocate that in such a condition, there may be five possible devices for successful communication. Firstly, mutual understanding between the speaker and the hearer. Secondly, job orientations among the person. Thirdly, motivations and propensities of the hearer. Fourthly, the intention of the speaker. And fifthly, the force, intonation, cadence and pitch of an utterance.

In addition to this, I have also elucidated the role of non-verbal speech act in communication. Indeed, when the speaker uses his utterance, he wants that the hearer not only understands his communicated intention but also he recognizes the speaker's intention, otherwise he will fail in communicating something. I advocate that if *securing of uptakes* is indispensable for communication, as Austin conceived, then it can be done non-verbally also. In every walk of life, the role of non-verbal speech act is displayed and received by us. If we shrug off the role of non-verbal speech act, we can't deem the correct meaning of an utterance of the speaker. I have, therefore, argued and elaborated that the speech act may be of three sorts: *Direct speech act, Indirect speech act,* and *Non-verbal speech act.*

Philosophers should not only study the nature and applications of language but also the relation of intention with language and behaviour. Language is merely a vehicle to express our ideas, thoughts and intentions. In all likelihood, the speaker may hide his real intention in language and express some intention which the speaker is like to wrongly convey. How the hearer judges the real intention of the speaker is a problem analysed in this book. I have argued that there would not be only one touchstone and method which may help the hearer to clearly understand the real intention of the speaker. Characteristics of behaviour and the context may provide more dependable cues to judge the real intention of the speaker. A speaker may hide his real intention in language but it is very difficult to hide it in varied nuances of behaviours. Even some trained actors fail to hide their real intentions in their behaviours. Hence, I conclude that the non-verbal actions, *i.e.,* behaviours are more accurate device to judge the intention of the speaker *inter alia* the other touchstones.

# Bibliography


Alston, W.O., and Natnnikhian, G. (Ed.) (1963). *Readings in Twentieth Century Philosophy.* The Free Press of Glencoe, London.

Alston, W.P. (1964). *Philosophy of Language.* Prentice-Hall, Inc, London.

Altieri, C. (1981). *Act and Quality*: A Theory of Liberty Meaning and Humanistic Understanding. The Harvester Press.

Anscombe, G.E.M. (1957). *Intention.* Blackwell.

Austin, J.L. (1962). *Sense and Sensibilia.* Edited by G.J. Warnock. Oxford University Press, London.

Austin, J.L. (1979). *Philosophical Papers.* Edited by G.J. Warnock and J.O. Urmson. Oxford University Press, London.

Austin, J.L. (1980). *How to Do Things with Words.* Edited by J.O. Urmson and Marina Sbisa. Oxford University Press, London.

Ayer, A.J. (1956). *The Problem of Knowledge.* Penguin Books: Baltimore.

Ayer, A.J. (1956). *The Revolution in Philosophy.* Macmillan and Co. Ltd.; London.

Ayer, A.J. (1958). *Language, Truth and Logic.* Gollanz, London.

Ayer, A.J. (1984). *Philosophy in Twentieth Century.* Counter point, Unwin Paper book, London.

Bach, K. (1987). *Thought and Reference.* Oxford University Press, Oxford.

Bach, K., and Hernish, R.M. (1979). *Linguistic Communication and Speech Acts.* M.I.T. Press, Cambridge.

Bakhle, S.W. (1987). Nature and Development of Linguistic Analysis. Dattsons, Nagpur.

Bennett, J. (1976). *Linguistic Behaviour.* Cambridge University Press, London.

Benveniste, E. (1966). *Problems de Linguistique Generala.* Paris: Gallimard.

Berlin, I. (1973). *Essays on J.L. Austin.* Clarendon Press, Oxford.

Berrendonner, A. (1982). *Elements de Pragmatique Linguistique.* Parris: Minuit.

Black, M. (Ed.) (1950). *Philosophical Analysis.* Cornell University Press, New York.

Blackburn, S. (1984). *Spreading the Word: Groundings in the Philosophy of Language.* Clarendon Press, Oxford.

Borgmann, A. (1974). *The Philosophy of Language: Historical Foundations and Contemporary Issues.* Martinus Nijhoff: The Hague.

Bowerman, M. (1981). *Language Development.* In H.C. Triandis and Alastair Heron (Eds.), Handbook of Cross-Cultural Philosophy, Development Philosophy, Vol. 4, Allyn and Bacon, Inc. Boston.

Brown, P. and Levinson, S. (1978). *Universals in Language Usage: Politeness Phenomena.* Cambridge University Press.

Carnap, R. (1937). *The Logical Syntax of Language.* Kegan Paul, London.

Carnap, R. (1942). *Introduction to Semantics.* Mass: Harvard University Press, Cambridge.

Cartwright, R. (1962). *Propositions.* In R.J. Butler (Ed.), Analytical Philosophy, Basil Blackwell, Oxford.

Cavell, S. (1976). *Must We Mean What We Say?* A Book of Essays. Cambridge University Press, London.

Chappell, V.C. (1964). *Ordinary Language.* Prentice-Hall, Inc, London.

Charlton, W. (1991). *The Analytic Ambition*: An Introduction to Philosophy. Basil Blackwell, Oxford.

Chisholm, R.M. (1966). *Theory of Knowledge.* Prentice-Hall, Englewood Cliffs, New Jersey.

Chomsky, N. (1985). *Aspects of the Theory of Syntax.* The M.I.T. Press, Cambridge, Massachusetts.

Connor, D.J.O. (Ed.) (1964). *A Critical History of Western Philosophy.* The Free Press of Glencoe, Collier-MacMillan Lt., London.

Copy, I.M., and Cohen, C. (1995). *An Introduction to Logic.* Prentice-Hall of India Private Limited, New Delhi.

Copleston, F. (1956). *Contemporary Philosophy.* Burnes and Oates, London.

Datta, D.M. (1970). *The Chief Currents of Contemporary Philosophy.* Calcutta University Pess, Calcutta.

Drtony, A. (Ed.) (1993). *Metaphor and Thought.* Cambridge University Press, New York.

Dummett, M. (1973). *Frege: Philosophy of Language.* Duckworth, London.

Diwedi, D.N. (1977). *Studies of Wittgenstein's Philosophy.* Darshan Peeth, Allahabad.

Ernest, L., and Gulick, R.V. (Eds.) (1991). *John Searle and His Critics.* Basil Blackwell Ltd., Oxford.

Fann, K.T. (Ed.) (1969). *Symposium on J.L. Austin.* Routledge and Kegan Paul, London.

Feigl, H., Sellers (Ed.) (1949). *Readings in Philosophical Analysis.* Appleton Cent. Craft, New York.

Fodor, J. (1975). *The Language of Thought.* Thomas Crowell, New York.

Fodor, J.A. and Katz, J.J. (1964). *The Structure of Language: Reading in the Philosophy of Language.* Prentice-Hall, Inc, Englewood Cliffs.

Furberg, M. (1969). *Locutionary and Illocutionary Acts*: A Main Theme in J.L. Austin's Philosophy. Toronto, Canada.

Furberg, M. (1971). *Saying and Meaning.* Basil Blackwell, Oxford.

Gardiner, A.H. (1932). *The Theory of Speech and Language.* Clarendon Press, London.

Gellner, E. (1960). *Words and Things*: A Critical Account of Linguistic Philosophy. Boston: Becon Press.

Goodman, N. (1949). *Likeness of Meaning.* In L. Linsky (Ed.), Semantics and the Philosophy of Language, (reprinted) University of Illinois Press, Urbana.

Grice, H.P. (1989). *Studies in the Way of Words.* Harvard University Press, Cambridge, Mass.

Hare, R.M. (1952). *The Language of Morals.* Oxford University Press, London.

Harrison, B. (1988). *An Introduction to the Philosophy of Language.* Macmillan Education.

Holdcroft, D. (1978). *Words and Deeds.* Clarendon Press, Oxford.

Katz, J.J. (1966). *The Philosophy of Language.* Harper and Row Publishers, New York.

Katz, J.J. (1972). *Semantic Theory.* Harper and Row, New York.

Katz, J.J. (1977). *Propositional Structure and Illocutionary Force.* Crowell, New York.

Katz, J.J., Postal, P.M. (1964). *An Integrated Theory of Linguistic Descriptions.* Mass.: M.I.T. Press, Cambridge.

Klibansky, R. (Ed.) (1968). *Contemporary Philosophy.* La Nuava Italia: Florence.

Lazerowitz, M. (1977). *The Language and Philosophy:* Freud and Wittgenstein. D. Reidel: Dordrecht, Holland.

Lemmon, E.J. (1966). *Sentences, Statements and Propositions.* In B.A.O. Williams and A.C. Monteflore (Ed.), British Analytical Philosophy, Routledge and Kegan Paul, London.

Lewis, D. (1986). *Convention: A Philosophical Study.* Billing and Sons Ltd., Worcester, U.K.

Lewis, H.D. (Ed.) (1956). *Contemporary British Philosophy.* (3rd Series). George Allen and Unwin Ltd., London.

Linsky, L. (Ed.) (1970). *Semantics and the Philosophy of Language.* University of Illinois Press, Urbana.

Lyas, C. (1972). *Philosophy and Linguistics.* Macmillan, St. Martin's Press, London.

Lyons, J. (1977). *Semantics.* Cambridge University Press, London.

Macdonald, M. (Ed.) (1954). *Philosophy and Analysis.* Basil Blackwell, Oxford.

Margalit, A. (1979). *Meaning and Use.* The Magnes Press. Jerusalem.

Martimich, A. (Ed.) (1985). *The Philosophy of Language.* Oxford University Press, New York.

Mathrani, G.N. (1990). *Studies in Wittgenstein Philosophy.* Darshana Peeth, Allahabad.

McCowley (1968). *Lexical Insertion in Transformational Grammar without Structure.* In papers of the Chicago Linguistic Society, Chicago.

Milligam, K. (Ed.) (1987). *Speech Act and Sachverhalt: Reinach and Foundations of Realist Phenomenology*. Martinus Nighoff Publishers, Dordrecht, Boston.

Millar, A. (2004): *Philosophy of Language*, Routledge, London.

Moore, G.E. (1922). *Philosophical Studies*. Routledge and Kegan Paul Ltd., London.

Moore, G.E. (1953). *Some Main Problems of Philosophy*. The Macmillan Co., New York.

Moore, G.E. (1959). *Philosophical Papers*. George Allen and Unwin, London.

Mooris, C.W. (1946). *Signs, Language and Behaviour*. N.J.: Prentice-Hall, Englewood Cliffs.

Muirhead, J.H. (Ed.) (1924-25). *Contemporary British Philosophy*. (1st and 2nd Series). George Allen and Unwin Ltd., London.

Mundle, C.W.K. (1979). *A Critique of Linguistic Philosophy*. Gloveer and Blain Limited, Kings Place, London.

Ortony, A. (Ed.) (1978). *Metaphor and Thought*. Cambridge University Press.

Pap, A. (1972). *The Element of Analytical Philosophy*. Hafner, New York.

Parkinson, G.H.R. (1970). *The Theory of Meaning*. Oxford University Press.

Passmore, J. (1984). *A Hundred Years of Philosophy*. Penguin Books, England.

Pears, D.F. (1966). *Wittgenstein and Austin*. In B. Williams and A. Monstefiore (Eds.), British Analytical Philosophy. Routledge and Kegan Paul, London.

Pitcher, G. (1985). *The Philosophy of Wittgenstein*. Prentice-Hall of India Private Limited, New Delhi.

Pitcher, G. (Ed.) (1968). *Wittgenstein*. Mac-Millan, London.

Pitcher, G.W. (1964). *Truth*. Englewood Cliffs, NJ, Prentice-Hall.

Platts, M. (1979): *Ways of Meaning*, Routledge and Kegan Paul, London.

Prasad, R. (1989). *Regularity, Normativity and Rules of Language and Other Essays in Philosophical Analysis*. The Poona University Press, Ganeshkhind, Poona.

Recanati, F. (1980). *Some remarks on Explicit Performatives, Indirect Speech Acts, Locutionary Meaning and Truth Value*. In J.R. Searle, F. Kiefer and M. Biermierch (Eds.) Speech Act Theory and Pragmatics, Reidel, Dordrecht, Holland.

Recanati, F. (1987). *Meaning and Force*: The Pragmatics of Performative Utterances. Cambridge University Press, London.

Richard, R. (1970). *The Linguistic Turn*. University of Chicago Press, Chicago.

Richards, I.A. (1965). *The Philosophy of Rhetoric*. Oxford University Press, New York.

Rosenberg, J.F. and Travis (1971). *Reading in the Philosophy of Language*, Prentice-Hall, Inc, New Jersey, U.S.A.

Runes, D. (Ed.) (1943). *Twentieth century Philosophy*. Philosophical Library, New York.

Russell, B. (1912). *The Problems of Philosophy*. Home University Library.

Russell, B. (1914). *Our Knowledge of External World*. Allen and Unwin, London.

Russell, B. (1921). *An Analysis of Mind*. Allen and Unwin, London.

Ryle, G. (1980). *Ordinary Language Analysis*. In G. Runkle (Ed.), Theory and Practice: An Introduction to Philosophy, Holt, Rinehart and Winston, New York.

Ryle, G. (Ed.) (1956). *The Revolution in Philosophy*. St. Martin Press, New York.

Sadock, J. (1974). *Toward a Linguistic Theory of Speech Acts*. Academic Press, New York.

Sampson, G. (1979). *Liberty and Language*. Oxford University Press, Oxford.

Schiffer, S.R. (1974). *Meaning*. Clarendon Press, London.

Searle, J.R. (1969). *Speech Acts: An essay in the Philosophy of Language*. Cambridge University Press.

Searle, J.R. (1979). *Expression and Meaning: Studies in the Theory of Speech Acts*. Cambridge University Press, New York, U.S.A.

Searle, J.R. (1983). *Intentionality: An essay in the Philosophy of Mind*. Cambridge University Press, New York, U.S.A.

Searle, J.R. (Ed.) (1979). *The Philosophy of Language.* Oxford University Press, London.

Searle, J.R. and Venderveken, D. (1985). *Foundations of Illocutionary Logic.* Cambridge University Press, New York, U.S.A.

Searle, J.R., Kiefer, F., and Bewitch, M. (Eds.) (1980). *Speech Act Theory and Pragmatics.* D. Reidel: Dordrecht, Holland.

Sears, D.O. *et al.* (1988). *Social Psychology.* Prentice-Hall, Englewood Cliffs, New Jersey, U.S.A.

Segerdahl, P. (1996). *Language Use: A Philosophical Investigation into the Basic Notions of Pragmatics.*

Stenius, E. (1960). *Wittgenstein's Tractatus.* Basil Blackwell and Mott Ltd.

Strawson, P. F. (1977). *Logico-Linguistic Papers.* Methuen and Co. Ltd., U.K.

Travis, C. (1975). *Saying and Understanding.* Blackwell. Oxford.

Urmson, J.O. (1966). *Philosophical Analysis.* Clarendon Press, London.

Warnock, G.J. (1958). *English Philosophy Since 1900.* Oxford University Press, London.

Warnock, G.J. (1989). *J.L. Austin.* Routledge, London and New York.

Weitz, M. (Ed.) (1966). *Twentieth Century Philosophy: The Analytic Tradition.* Free Press, New York.

White, A.R. (1958). *G.E. Moore: A Critical Exposition.* Oxford Blackwell and Mott Ltd.

White, M. (Ed.) (1955). *The Age of Analysis.* Mentor Books, New York.

Wittgenstein, L. (1953). *Philosophical Investigations.* Edited by G.E.M. Anscombe and R. Rhees. Translated by G.E.M. Anscombe, Basil Blackwell and Mott Ltd., London.

Wittgenstein, L. (1959). *The Blue and Brown Books.* Basil Blackwell and Mott Ltd., London.

Wittgenstein, L. (1961). *Tractatus-Logico-Philosophicus.* Translated by D.F. Peers and B.F. Mcguinness, London Routledge and Kegan Paul, New York.

Wunderlich, D. (1979). *Foundations of Linguistics.* Translated by Roger Lass. Cambridge University Press. London.

## Articles

Alston, W.O. (1964). *Linguistic Acts.* American Philosophical Quarterly.

Anderson, P.D. (1995). *Imperative Frames and Modality: Direct Vs. Indirect Speech Acts in Russian, Danish and English.* Linguistic and Philosophy.

Armstrong, D.M. (1971). *Meaning and Communication.* Philosophical Review.

Bach, K. (1975). *Performatives Are Statements Too.* Philosophical Review.

Bach, K. (1992). *How Performatives Really Work: A Reply to Searle.* Linguistic and Philosophy.

Bach, K. (1995). *Standardization and Conventionalization.* Linguistic and Philosophy.

Carr, C.R. (1980). *A Speech Act Dilemma.* Analysis.

Chisholm, R.M. (1951). *Philosophers and Ordinary Language.* Philosophical Review.

Cooper, D.E. (1972). *Meaning and Illocution.* American Philosophical Quarterly.

Davidson, A. (1975). *Indirect Speech Acts and What To Do With Them.* Syntax and Semantics.

Davis, S. (1979). *Perlocutions.* Linguistic and Philosophy.

Dorschel, A. (1987). *What Is It To Understand A Directive Speech Act?* Indian Philosophical Quarterly.

Fingarette, H. (1967). *Performative.* American Philosophical Quarterly.

Fraser, B. (1975). *Hedged Performatives.* Syntax and Semantics.

Garner, R.T. (1970). *Some doubt about Illocutionary Negation.* Analysis.

Geach, P. (1965). *Assertion.* Philosophical Review.

Ginet, C. (1979). *Performativity, Linguistic and Philosophy.*

Green, G.M. (1973). *How To Get People To Do Things With Words.* (Reprinted). Syntax and Semantics.

Green, O.H. (1968). *Intentions and Speech Acts. Analysis.*

Grice, H.P. (1957). *Meaning. Philosophical Review.*

Grice, H.P. (1969). *Utterer's Meaning and Intention.* Philosophical Review.

Hajdin, M. (1991). *Is There More To Speech Acts Than Illocutionary Force And Propositional Content?* Nous.

Hare, R.M. (1970). *Meaning and Speech Acts.* Philosophical Review.

Hedenius, I. (1963). *Performatives,* Theoria.

Hughes, J. (1984). *Group Speech Acts. Linguistic and Philosophy.*

Kuroda, S.Y. (1986). *A Formal Theory of Speech Acts.* Linguistic and Philosophy.

Lemmon, E.J. (1962). *On Sentences Verifiable by Their Use.* Analysis.

Morgan, J.L. (1978). *Two Types of Convention in Indirect Speech Acts.* Syntax and Semantics.

Nordenstam, T. (1966). *On Austin's Theory of Speech Act.* Mind.

Phaharaj, D.M. (1995). *Speech Acts: As Linguistic Communicative Function.* Indian Philosophical Quarterly.

Raphael, D.D. (1956). *Linguistic Performative of Descriptive Meaning.* Mind.

Reimer, M. (1995). *Performative Utterances: A Reply to Bach and Hernish.* Linguistic and Philosophy.

Reinhardt, L.R. (1967). *Proposition and Speech Acts.* Mind.

Rieber, S. (1997). *Conventional Implicatures As Tacit Performatives.* Linguistic and Philosophy.

Samek, R. (1965). *Performative Utterances and the Concept of Contract.* Australasian Journals of Philosophy.

Searle, J.R. (1962). *Meaning and Speech Acts.* Philosophical Review.

Searle, J.R. (1968). *Austin on Locutionary and Illocutionary Acts.* Philosophical Review.

Searle, J.R. (1975). *Indirect Speech Acts.* In P. Cole and J.L. Morgan (Eds.), *Syntax and Semantics,* Vol. 3, Speech Acts. Academic Press.

Searle, J.R. (1975). *Indirect Speech Acts.* Syntax and Semantics.

Searle, J.R. (1989). *How Performatives Work.* Linguistic and Philosophy.

Skjei, E. (1985). *A Comment on Performative,* Subject and Proposition in Habermas's Theory of Communication. Inquiry.

Teichman, J. (1961). *Propositions.* Philosophical Review.

Thaw, S. (1971). *The Distinction Between Rhetic and Illocutionary Acts.* Analysis.

Tsohatzidis, S.L. (1987). *Deontic trouble in Speech Act Botany.* Analysis.

Turner, R. (1985). *Speech and Social Contract.* Inquiry.

Warnock, G.J. (1971). *Hare on Meaning and Speech Acts.* Philosophical Review.

White, A.R. (1962). *Review of How to Do Things with Words.* Analysis.

White, A.R. (1965). *Review of Mats Furberg's Locutionary and Illocutionary Acts,* Mind.

Wright, M. (1965). *I Know and Performative Utterances.* Australasian Journals of Philosophy.

# Index